LEVERAGE YOUR EXPERTISE

HOW TO SCALE UP, CREATE IMPACT AND LIVE THE LIFESTYLE YOU DESIRE.

BY MATTHEW MASON

First published by Ultimate World Publishing 2022
Copyright © 2022 Matthew Mason

ISBN

Paperback: 978-1-922828-32-3
Ebook: 978-1-922828-33-0

Matthew Mason has asserted his rights under the Copyright, Designs and Patents Act 1988 to be identified as the author of this work. The information in this book is based on the author's experiences and opinions. The publisher specifically disclaims responsibility for any adverse consequences which may result from use of the information contained herein. Permission to use information has been sought by the author. Any breaches will be rectified in further editions of the book.

All rights reserved. No part of this publication may be reproduced, stored in or introduced into a retrieval system, or transmitted in any form, or by any means (electronic, mechanical, photocopying, recording or otherwise) without the prior written permission of the author. Any person who does any unauthorised act in relation to this publication may be liable to criminal prosecution and civil claims for damages. Enquiries should be made through the publisher.

Cover design: Ultimate World Publishing
Layout and typesetting: Ultimate World Publishing
Editor: Vanessa McKay

Ultimate World Publishing
Diamond Creek,
Victoria Australia 3089
www.writeabook.com.au

DEDICATION

For the loves of my life Kathleen, Cameron and Caitlin.

CONTENTS

◆◇◆

DEDICATION..................................... iii

INTRODUCTION................................... 1

PART 1: BENEFITS OF LEVERAGING
YOUR EXPERTISE............................ 7

PART 2: THE TWO KEY FACTORS 13

PART 3: OUR BLUE OCEAN FORMULA 19

PART 4: THE 7 STEPS TO THE BLUE OCEAN 55

CONCLUSION 129

PART X: MY STORY............................. 131

ABOUT THE AUTHOR 135

ACKNOWLEDGEMENTS 137

WORK WITH ME................................. 139

INTRODUCTION

INTRODUCTION

WHO IS THIS BOOK FOR?

Do you have knowledge in your head, information in a book, or great experience in an area? Are you an expert sitting on a mountain of knowledge, struggling to unpack it into a product to share with the world? Do you want to leverage your expertise and add value to your business?

If yes, then read on.

This book is for people wanting to become edupreneurs (educational entrepreneurs). Someone looking to create value through the delivery of educational products or services. Someone taking their years' of experience and knowledge and unpacking that into a learning product that can provide value and impact people.

Some questions to consider if you are an edupreneur.

- Do you have several years' experience in a topic or area?

- Do you have a particular methodology or framework that you use that is going to provide value to others to make it easier or better for them to complete their tasks?

- Do you have a desire to share your knowledge, to create impact and change in the world?

Answering yes to these questions suggests you are on the path to becoming an edupreneur. In this book I will show you how to leverage your expertise through digital learning experiences and add value to your business.

INTRODUCTION

THE GROWING ONLINE LEARNING MARKET

It's never been easier to learn something new. The internet provides a huge wealth of resources, making it possible to soak up information that simply wouldn't have been available in the past. Previously, connections were too slow for video downloads, and content streaming was simply impossible. Distance learning companies have always existed, but it wasn't until they could start using the web effectively that they grew.

The Australian online education market stood at around four billion dollars in 2018. It is anticipated to grow at a compound annual growth rate of over eight percent and exceed seven billion dollars by 2024. This is due to technological advancements, eager learners and increasing use of smart devices (Research & Markets, 2019). These figures show that the perceptions surrounding online learning have shifted. You can find online courses on just about every topic, and many traditional schools now offer their own versions of online courses.

The future is bright for online learning, and this field isn't slowing soon. The courses you can find and how they are delivered are constantly improving as time goes on, with more and more professionals looking for ways to provide their clients with innovative, scalable and cost-effective experiences.

COVID affected traditional face-to-face training in a way the industry has never seen, with many coaches, consultants and facilitators embracing the benefits that digital learning provides. Educators saw the positive impact of spacing learning rather than cramming it all into a day or two of face-to-face training. Online learning is more focused, provides the solution to a single problem, and has a greater impact. Eduprenuers saw how they could scale their offering, beyond their normal reach, for greater visibility and profitability.

This provides the authors, thought leaders and entrepreneurs with an opportunity to deliver their content online, to create superb digital learning experiences and a scalable and impactful offering. It provides an opportunity to create not just another revenue stream for their business, but potentially a highly profitable offering that could provide 50% or more business income.

PART 1

BENEFITS OF LEVERAGING YOUR EXPERTISE

———————— ◆◇◆ ————————

In the previous chapter, we touched on some of the huge benefits with leveraging expertise, but let's explore these in more detail.

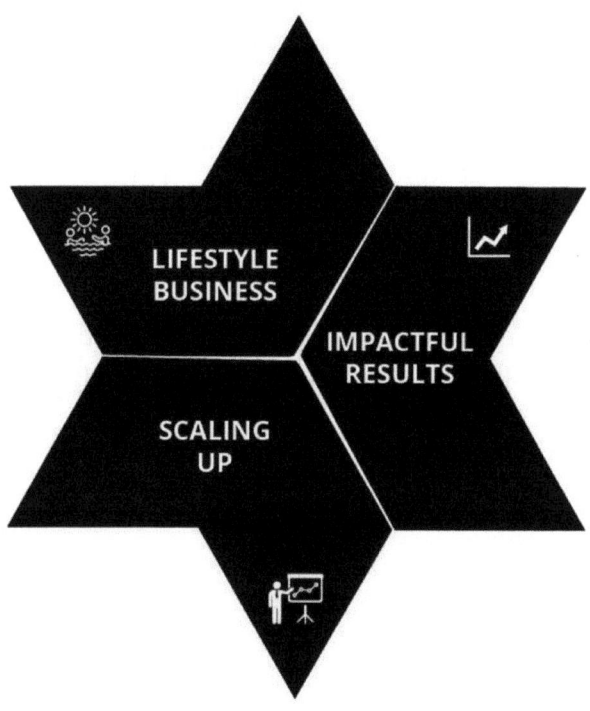

IMPACTFUL RESULTS

The first big benefit is **impactful results.**

Taking the information in your head and leveraging that valuable expertise through digital learning assets to be consumed anywhere, anytime, means that you can reach more people and create a greater impact.

By spending less time delivering information, you can spend more time delivering transformation. And this is where the real impact can be provided. Working with your clients, solving the problems the information assets don't solve, helping them transform and get actual results.

The Pareto principle is very relevant to coaching or training situations. It states that 80% of consequences come from 20% of the causes. When helping people get results, to truly transform, we find that 80% of the results come from 20% of the training or coaching activities. If you can increase the time that you deliver that 20% (because the other 80% is now being delivered through the leveraged digital learning assets) then you're going to create a bigger impact. This is going to create some huge, magnificent, impactful results.

SCALING UP

The next big benefit is **scalability**. Creating digital learning assets and delivering them through an online course allows you to scale. The delivery of a face-to-face class can fit 20-30 people. If you are doing a large event, you might deliver to 100 plus people. Delivering a workshop virtually allows you to deliver to many. But these events are one point in time and require you as the key person to deliver.

Without leveraging your expertise into digital assets, there is a limitation. You can only scale as much as you're physically able to deliver. Digital learning assets, delivered through an online course, give you the ability to scale across to thousands or more people and reach them in different ways. Enriching them in ways that are suitable for them and their preference for learning.

The key element to scaling is having the assets in place. You are one asset, but you need to create other assets that can share your expertise to allow for that scale to happen. Otherwise, you are limited. Without those assets, you will not scale.

You could scale to an extent with other physical assets. This could include upskilling other coaches to deliver your programs on your behalf. However, this is still limited physically. No coach is ever going to be available 24/7 365 days a year. In addition, while this will allow you to scale your client numbers, it is not going to have a corresponding scale in your profit margin.

Digital learning assets allow for that scale to occur. People can access your information anytime, anywhere. Digital delivery allows for a greater profit margin. There is less outlay, fewer costs, and therefore higher profit margins.

LIFESTYLE BUSINESS

The major benefit of leveraging your expertise is that you will have a **lifestyle business**. Your signature solution that leverages your expertise will be operating at scale and generating high profits. This will allow you to work the hours that you want to work, from the location you love while having the lifestyle that you desire.

This lifestyle can be whatever you desire. As you scale and reach more people and generate higher profits, you will have so many more choices.

You can choose to continue to deliver your programs at a high profit margin, which is going to allow you to live a more affluent lifestyle. However, you may also choose to live a lifestyle that gives something back. You may choose to divert some of your profits into a social enterprise that is going to assist those less fortunate.

> To achieve our goal of giving, we have partnered with B1G1 to become a Business for Good. By partnering with the B1G1 Global Giving Initiative, we form a direct link between the work we do and how much we give back.
>
> B1G1 enables us to give to a good cause during our daily business, helping to affect change where it is needed and make a positive impact on the world.
>
> Mavenzeal is proudly committed to the United Nations Sustainable Development Global Goals. We strive towards the UN Goal #4 of "Quality Education to ensure inclusive and equitable quality education and promote lifelong learning opportunities for all."
>
> In fact, for every copy of this book that we sell, we provide educational resources for seriously ill children in Australia.

Alternatively, you may choose to lower your fees to provide more access to your online courses. By doing that, you are giving the opportunity for learning to those that are slightly disadvantaged and rarely have the income to access that knowledge.

LEVERAGE YOUR EXPERTISE

Leverage through the digital learning assets that is generating a higher profit for you means you can choose to work less. You no longer have to work 40 or 50 hours a week (like many business owners), now that so much of your information is being delivered and consumed while you are doing other things. This is going to allow you to spend more time with family, friends, loved ones, and not being so consumed with the work that you are doing.

PART 2

THE TWO KEY FACTORS

———————————— ◆◇◆ ————————————

There are two key factors that really determine the results you're getting and how successful you are at delivering impact, scaling the business, and living the lifestyle you desire.

The first factor depends on the volume of clients or the volume of work you have coming in. This can scale between a low volume and a high volume. Ideally, we would want to have a high volume of clients. However, how we manage that volume and the amount of work we must do depends on the other key factor.

The other factor is how you are delivering your programs. One to one or delivering one to many. If all your time is spent working with an individual client or working one-to-some with smaller groups, you are going to be physically limited in how many clients you can serve. If you have scaled by leveraging your expertise through digital learning assets, you will easily be delivering one-to-many.

It is these two factors that determine the results that you are getting and how scalable the business is.

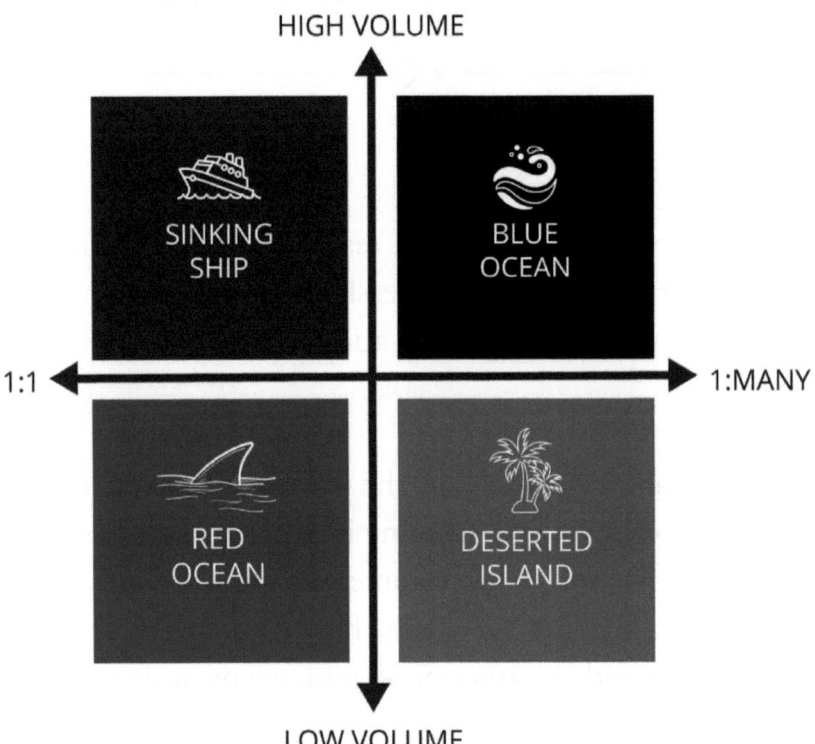

THE RED OCEAN

Businesses that are delivering one to one and have a low volume of clients are sitting in the **Red Ocean**. It's red from the blood in the water from the sharks and the competition. You are trading your time for money, competing on price, and offering discounts. Effectively in a race to the bottom.

THE TWO KEY FACTORS

I know I've been there. When you first start out in business, you are trying to make a name for yourself. If you don't have runs on the board, previous clients that can recommend you or proven results with your signature solution, if you don't have something that really allows you to stand out, then you are competing with other people in the same space. There is also a level of desperation, with a desire to get clients. Often you are left in a position where to compete you need to reduce your fees. Unfortunately, your competition may do the same and effectively it becomes this race to the bottom.

THE SINKING SHIP

One of the best ways to move out of the red ocean is by increasing the volume of clients.

However, if you are not leveraging your expertise, as the volume of clients increase, while still delivering one-to-one, you end up doing a lot more work. You struggle to service a higher volume of clients one-to-one, as the workload increases. That effectively puts you on what we call the **Sinking Ship**.

When I started my business, one thing I did it for was for the lifestyle. I wanted the freedom to choose the hours I worked. To spend time with my family, to have the flexibility of doing things when I wanted.

But unfortunately, I got onto the sinking ship, and all of that went away. I ended up working much longer hours. I was working 40, 50, or maybe even more hours. Working until stupid o'clock at night. Working on the weekends just to deliver the service that was needed for the volume of clients I had, to have to stay out of that red ocean.

This can lead to burn out because you're doing so much . Or the quality suffers, which then means that you lose clients. As the service quality drops, the volume of clients drops off and they fall back into the Red Ocean, or simply go down with their Sinking Ship.

THE DESERTED ISLAND

The alternative is to move away from the one-to-one, towards a one-to-many model. However, if you still have a low volume of clients, then you move onto the **Deserted Island**.

You become an untapped resource of value that no one knows about. You've potentially got a great product or service that you can provide, but you are sitting on this deserted island because few people know about you or your program. You are trying to scale. Trying to deliver one to many, but you don't have the volume of clients that's needed. You are not standing out enough to be noticed and generate the volume of clients you need.

THE TWO KEY FACTORS

THE BLUE OCEAN

The ideal situation to be in, is the **Blue Ocean**. This is where you are away from the red ocean. Away from the sharks and the competition, where you're able to stand up, get noticed and scale.

This is where you have leveraged your expertise, created digital learning assets, allowing you to deliver one to many, and generating the ideal volume of clients. This puts you into the Blue Ocean of calm, away from the stress and competition. Letting you live the lifestyle you desire. You are no longer competing on price. You have probably leveraged that expertise through a signature method that you are now delivering to many through online courses and virtual coaching programs.

So how do we get there? Well, it's about implementing the six key pillars of the blue ocean formula. In the next chapter we are going to unpack each one of those pillars in more detail.

PART 3

OUR BLUE OCEAN FORMULA

———————————— ◆◇◆ ————————————

Creating a superb learning experience so you can create impact, scale, and live the lifestyle you love might seem like a faraway dream. But, if you implement the right strategies, you can get there far sooner than you think.

The Blue Ocean Formula that we have developed outlines these six key pillars you need to create impact, scale, and live the lifestyle you love.

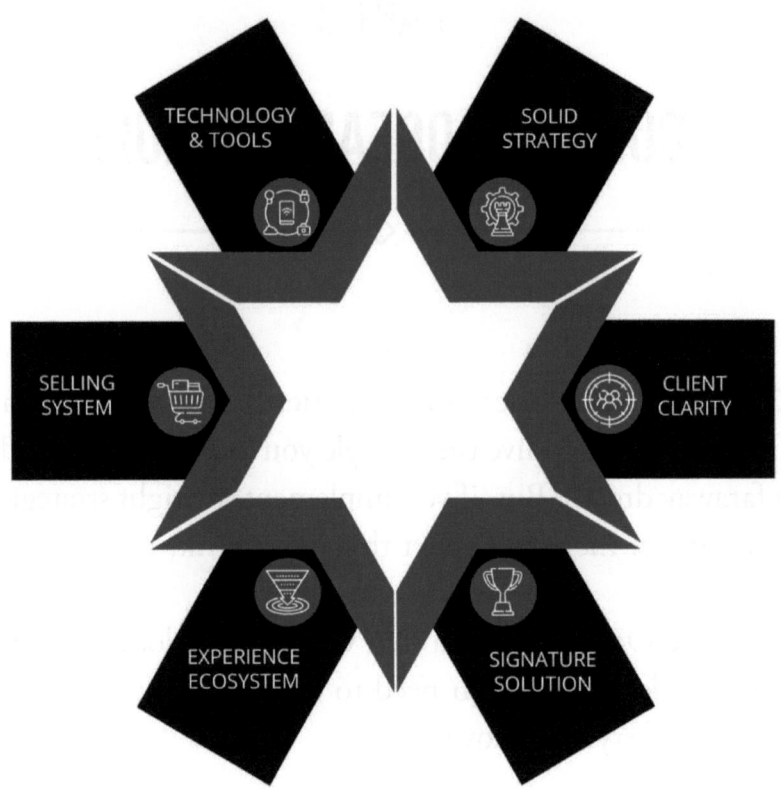

SOLID STRATEGY

If you're serious about creating impact, scaling and living the lifestyle you love, one of the first things you absolutely must do is to develop a solid strategy.

A solid strategy is necessary to understand where you want to go, the results you want to achieve, and the market you want to target. This is where we align your 'why' - your passion and profession - with the goals of your business.

Without a solid strategy the design and development of the digital learning assets, your courses and programs will be like a rudderless ship. There will be no direction and it will waste extensive time with design and development.

> *If you don't know where you are going, any road will get you there* – Cheshire Care, Alice in Wonderland

If you don't know what your strategy is, you are going to be drifting, and certainly not going to get into that blue ocean. You're going to be drifting around in the oceans if you don't have a clear and solid strategy. So, the three big things that we want to be looking at as part of this strategy is the why, the where, and the what.

What is your why?

The first thing to consider is the why. Why are you wanting to leverage your expertise and create digital learning assets? As we have explored, there are several benefits, but you really need to get clear around which of those benefits tap into your why. Because the reason you are doing it is going to impact on what you are actually creating.

If your why is focused on creating profit, to have a passive income that suits the lifestyle you desire, which involves you working as little as possible, then you're going to be focused on building a self-paced online course that people are going to go through in their own time, without your involvement.

Whereas if your why is more focused on creating impact and delivering transformational change, then the experience you're going to create is going to be different.

You will still be leveraging your expertise through digital assets, but you are also going to be spending a lot of your time coaching and helping your clients to generate that transformational change.

Get clear on your why at the start, otherwise you are not going to create an experience that is aligned with your why, and if it is not aligned with your why, then it's not going to be fulfilling.

The edupreneurial sweet spot

The why directly relates to your purpose. When you look at successful entrepreneurs, you'll find that they are operating in that entrepreneurial sweet spot. That place where problem, product, passion and profit all intersect. To be successful as an edupreneur, you also need to find that sweet spot. Miss any of these factors and you are going to miss that edupreneurial sweet spot.

This sweet spot can also be likened to the Japanese concept of Ikigai. Ikigai means 'reason for being'. It refers to having a direction or purpose in life that makes one's life worthwhile.

In determining your sweet spot, you need to consider the following factors.

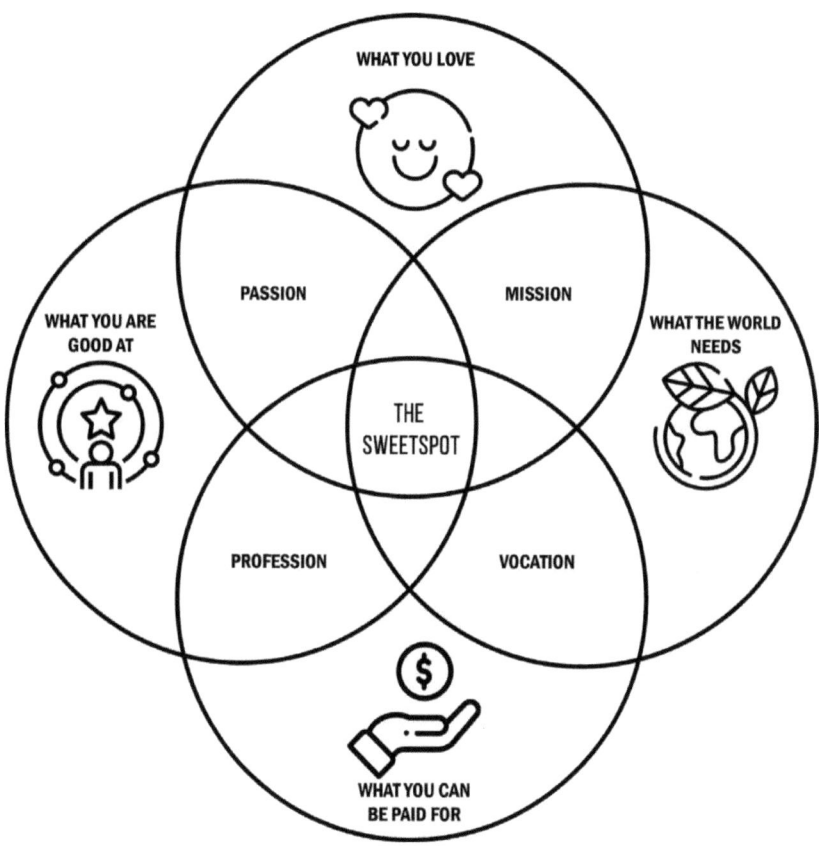

Passion

Having passion for the subject matter you are delivering is vital for the success of an edupreneur. Without passion, you are going to lack the motivation to put in the hard yards when needed. Procrastination has a greater chance of taking over or you become distracted by the new shiny objects when the design, development or delivery of the product becomes difficult. Passion is also essential to provide a superb learning experience to the people undertaking your program.

Problem
You need to be solving a problem. People don't pay for a course. They pay to have a problem solved. You need to make sure that you are delivering a solution to that problem. What is it that people in your world need and what can you do to solve this need?

Product
To be a successful edupreneur you need a product. The product is taking your subject matter expertise to solve the problem. This is converted into a learning experience that provides value to your learners. Many people have the expertise around the product but lack the capability to design and develop the learning experience. That element is less critical, as you can collaborate with learning designers (such as Mavenzeal) to receive the support and technical know-how required.

Profit
The final key factor is profit. Creating an income generating business through educational products. There needs to be a market for your learning program that will pay a price (preferably a premium one) to access your product that is going to deliver you a profit. The profit is generated once the revenue from sales is greater than the cost in design, developing and delivering the course. Profit is going to be

determined by price point and sales volume. You could look to create a profit through a low price point with a high volume of sales or a higher price point with a lower volume of sales.

Without **passion**, you are going to be an unmotivated educator that will never finish developing their course or building a lacklustre experience that fails to provide value.

Without an effective **product**, you will sell a course that fails to engage the audience and deliver on the promises provided.

Without solving a **problem**, you will have a product that you struggle to promote and sell.

Without profit, you are just a passionate educator, giving away your knowledge through an online product.

Where does it fit?

The second part of the **Solid Strategy** is where your online course, virtual coaching program or the digital learning assets fit into your existing business. Is it something that is going to compliment your existing business? Is it going to supplement your existing business? Or is it going to replace your existing business?

If you're delivering coaching programs, then putting your content together into digital assets that you can deliver anytime or anywhere is going to help you compliment what you offer your clients. It is going to allow you to spend more time delivering the desired transformation, to move your clients from problem to prize.

Digital assets, can supplement what you are already providing to your clients in your coaching calls, by providing them with a suite of digital learning assets (including templates and checklists) that they can refer back to, or use after the coaching calls.

Alternatively, you may want to change your business model and just go completely online.

What is your vision for success?

The final part of Solid Strategy is to understand what your vision for success is. This is where you want to define your champagne moment. This is looking at the point in time when you have achieved exactly what you want to achieve, and you have managed to transform and leverage your expertise in such a way that you are living the lifestyle that you desire.

It's about being really clear on the path that you need to take, the milestones you need to reach along the way, and the timeframe for reaching those milestones and the end goal. This is going to help you measure how you are going, but more importantly it will keep you on track and accountable to yourself.

CLIENT CLARITY

The second pillar of the Blue Ocean Formula is Client Clarity. It's about being very targeted in the selection of a niche and getting clear on your target audience. Then understanding the people in this niche that you're serving so you can provide a solution to their problem.

Define your niche

One key to finding success with any business starts with finding a paying market. Finding a niche that pays and then creating content, products, and services for that niche is the only way you will build a solid foundation for a successful online coaching or learning business.

A big problem that we often see is coaches, consultants, and facilitators trying to be across a broad range of industries. The truly successful ones, target a specific niche and are able to move out of the red ocean and create their own market in the blue ocean of calm.

> *When you try to be everything to everyone, you accomplish being nothing to anyone – Bonnie Gillespie*

Having a specific niche, increases your reach. This might sound a little counter intuitive to think about narrowing down to reach more. But narrowing your niche gives you the ability to be very targeted and very focused in solving a specific problem for a specific market. This allows you to target you marketing, and give you much better results.

For example, too broad a niche would be small business owners. This niche could include hairdressers, takeaway stores, marketing companies, personal trainers and any other business that provides a business or service that is classed as a small business. The problems that they are having will be quite varied.

A more targeted approach using a vertical or horizontal niche is preferable.

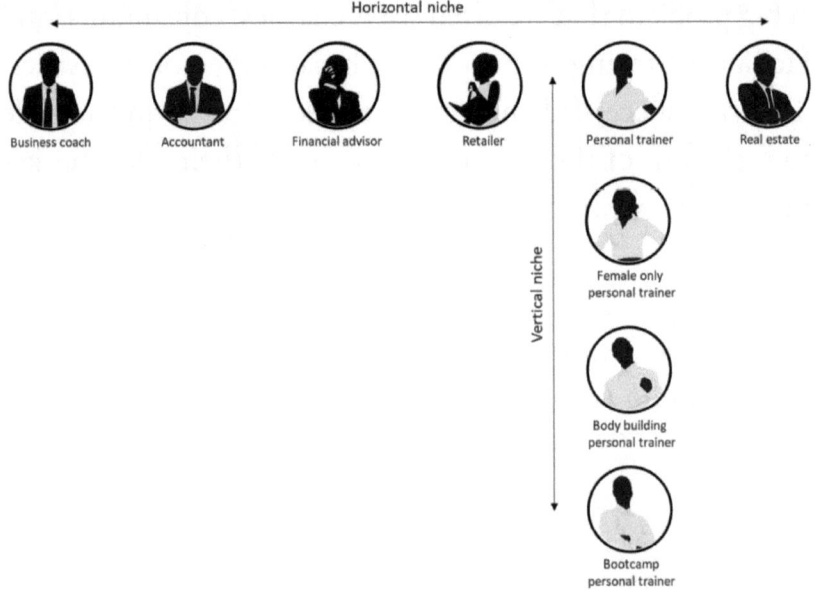

A vertical niche could be personal trainers. This group could be further defined as personal trainers that run bootcamps. You could then target this groups specific problems.

A horizontal niche could be small business owners with teams of two to ten people with an annual turnover of less than one million dollars. Here you would find common problems related to managing teams, onboarding the right staff, or scaling income beyond one million dollars.

Instead of having a scatter-gun approach and just throwing content out there and throwing marketing out there and trying to get anyone that is willing to work with you, you become more targeted through your specific niche. It provides you with a smaller target to aim for and allows you to be more specific with the problems you can solve.

You will become seen as the expert in this area. An expert in solving a specific problem.

Understanding the persona

You cannot deliver an effective user experience without a clear idea of who is going to be accessing your program. It is not just a case of putting content together but having a clear understanding of the client persona.

It is about putting yourself in your clients' shoes, so you can develop empathy for them. Then you are able to craft an experience that is ruthlessly relevant. Something that really taps into exactly what your clients need. If people can't see relevance in what they are doing, then they are going to struggle to apply that knowledge later. People are more engaged when they can see the WIIFM ('What's In It For Me').

To make the process of client clarity easier, I developed the PERSONAS Model. This includes looking at a basic profile, developing empathy for the user, exploring their reasons (or motivations), their skills, knowledge and experiences, obstacles to learning, their needs, and how they access technology.

We will explore this model in more details later in the book.

Solving a problem

The basic premise of all businesses is to solve a problem. Whether this is to provide a product or deliver a service, the end goal is to solve a problem that the client or customer has. Without client clarity, you won't know what their problems are, and you can't develop a solution to fix those problems.

People don't want to buy a drill bit, they want a hole. Focus on the problem to be solved when designing learning.

It is important to understand that people don't want to pay for your course, program, or service. They want to pay for the solution that you provide. They want a solution to the problem they have. They want something that takes their pain away. Once you clearly define your client, their problems, and their needs you can develop the painkiller solution they require.

SIGNATURE SOLUTION

Besides a solid strategy and client clarity, you need a signature solution if you are ever going to create impact, scale and live the lifestyle you love. This strategy is powerful because it can help you get the knowledge out of your head and allow you to leverage your expertise in a much shorter timeframe.

The reality is that the knowledge in your head is invaluable, but it is intangible. If it's in your head no one can take advantage of that value.

A signature solution packages your intellectual property into a product that easily expresses the outcome and value that you provide. It is the ideal vehicle for moving your business from trading time for money, working one-on-one, or delivering bespoke programs to a business that is scalable, has a greater impact and provides the lifestyle that you desire.

The problem we see with many coaches, consultants and facilitators (and many other service providers) is that they don't know how to share their knowledge in a way that establishes them as a thought leader, and they are left in the Red Ocean of competition.

The key thing they are lacking is a signature solution.

Building credibility

Creating a unique signature solution shows that you are enough of an expert to have developed a system to get the results that your clients need. It provides an instant boost to your credibility and allows you to attract the clients you want to serve. They can clearly see the results that your signature solution provides, and deciding to work with you becomes easy.

Creating your unique signature solution is a great way to get out of the Red Ocean of competition and sharks and move into the Blue Ocean of calm. No one else will have your signature solution so it allows you to make the competition irrelevant. You are no longer just a business coach or sales trainer. You become known as the person with your Signature Solution (whatever name you give it) that follows a defined process, using your knowledge and expertise to achieve the desired results and providing great benefits.

Building credibility in your niche, where you are known for your signature solution, will create many more opportunities for collaboration. People will want to work with you, because you have a solution to solve the problems of the client base that you share. You can enjoy the benefits of getting more attention, more referrals, and more business that collaboration provides.

Defined structure

Having a signature solution that you know works, gives you the framework to help your clients deliver amazing and impactful results. It provides a very defined process and clearly details the steps to take people from problem to prize. The framework allows you to have a very focused delivery, where you put people through a specific process focused on creating impact.

Your signature solution will instil greater confidence in your clients. By showing them the journey you are going to take them on, showing that you have a defined process to take them from problem to prize, you immediately instil a sense of confidence in your client. Confidence that you are the person to help, and solve their problems. Everyone loves a plan and having the confidence that you have a solid plan will make the decision to work with you so much easier.

Your signature solution is going to give you a sense of peace and sanity. No longer are you reinventing the wheel with every client. Having a solution with a defined process, clearly identifying the results and benefits you provide is going to streamline your business. It is going to reduce the amount of stress caused by a lack of time, inefficiencies in the business and low profit margins.

Your clients will love your signature solution and so will you, as it allows you to enjoy the value you are providing without the stress.

Delivering consistently

A signature solution provides consistency across many areas of your business.

The results you provide, the process to follow and the benefits of working with you are all clearly developed as part of your signature solution. This ensures that you have consistency in your messaging that you put onto social media, when talking with prospective clients, and in any of your marketing campaigns.

Consistency in messaging brings a consistent flow of clients. Your signature solution clearly displays the results you provide and, having confidence that you have a defined process to follow, you will be able to develop a consistent flow of clients that you want to work with.

With consistent messaging and clients comes a consistent cash flow. You will step off the cash flow roller coaster and be confident that you have the clients and cash flow coming in to allow you to live the lifestyle you desire.

EXPERIENCE ECOSYSTEM

The fourth pillar of the Blue Ocean Formula is the experience ecosystem.

A signature solution allows you to package your intellectual property into an ecosystem of experiences that you can deliver digitally. The reality is for people to work with you, they need to know like, and trust you. Creating an experience ecosystem allows for this to occur.

A funnel approach

An ecosystem allows for a funnel approach to the solution design, which is used to break down the client journey. The funnel approach takes the client from the interest stage, where they learn why the topic is important to them, through to the integration stage, where skills and knowledge are applied in the development of mastery. In between these stages, information and implementation products or programs can be delivered. From each of these stages, you can develop various learning experiences. These can be given away for free (to generate awareness in your brand), sold for a low cost, or sold as a high-ticket offer, where most of the profits will be made.

The funnel approach to the ecosystem can be divided into informational and transformational experiences.

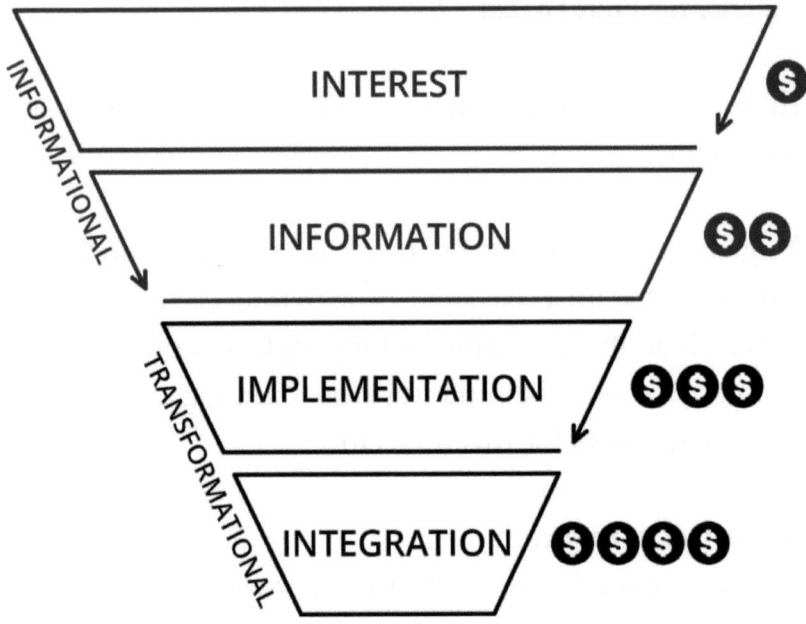

Informational Vs Transformational Experiences

The informational experiences are low (or no) cost products that are highly leveraged with people consuming them without your involvement.

The first level is interest experiences. These will help your target market and potential clients identify that they have a problem. Your interest experiences are going to help people become problem aware and let them know you have a solution to the problem. The interest experiences also let them find out more about you, your brand, and your solution.

The next level is information experiences. These are things like a minicourse or a five- day challenge. As the name suggests, they are experiences that provide the information on how to solve the problem. They provide the knowledge, but do not deliver an experience that provides the skills to solve the problem. You are not helping people with how to do something. You are just giving them the knowledge and saying, these are the things you need to do.

The next two levels are the transformational experiences. These are less leveraged and require more of your time to deliver. Transformation won't just happen through an online learning program, as people will still have questions and need assistance in how they can implement and integrate the learning into their own situation.

This is where your implementation experience comes in. This is going to require a higher investment from your client, but they will get more value out of the implementation products. The implementation product could be a self-paced online program that people can consume in their own time, combined with a Facebook community or coaching calls that takes your knowledge and allows you to deliver the transformation that is needed.

The last experience in the funnel is the integration experience. This is usually delivered as a one-on-one. This is a very low leveraged experience as it requires a lot of your skills and experience to help your client move beyond implementation to integrating the learning into their daily life or work practices.

High-ticket or low-ticket?

One of the big questions I often get asked, and see many others asking on forums and groups, is if they should develop and sell a high-ticket or low-ticket program.

There are arguments for both. If you are looking to scale and generate a large profit, then a high-ticket program is going to be the best way to do this. However, it is going to take more work to design and develop a high-ticket program that delivers value for money.

It will be much easier to sell a low-ticket program. In addition, the development of a low-ticket program will also be easier. However, you will need to sell a much larger volume to generate the same level of income.

An alternative is to develop a mid-ticket program that sits between the low and high-ticket offers.

Let's have a look at some figures to compare these options as stand-alone programs.

Program	Target	Cost	Sales required
Low-ticket (LT)	$20,000	$25	800
Mid-ticket (MT)	$20,000	$500	40
High-ticket (HT)	$20,000	$5,000	4

If you are looking to scale and generate good profits, then a high-ticket program is the way to go. A low-ticket program is not going to provide enough profit to build a scalable business. A mid-ticket program is also going to require a high volume of sales and marketing effort.

But it is going to be harder to sell a high-ticket program to a cold audience. A high-ticket offer is a bigger investment and often you will need something to attract their interest and provide an opportunity for them to know, like, and trust you. This is where the experience ecosystem comes in.

By using the experience ecosystem as a sales funnel, we can attract people into a low ticket offer and then upsell them into the higher programs.

Let's have a look at these options again, with some assumptions around the conversion rates.

Program	Cost	Sales	Income
Low-ticket (LT) *Interest product*	$25	200	$5,000
Mid-ticket (MT) *Information product*	$500	20 (10% convert from LT)	$10,000
High-ticket (HT) *Implementation product*	$5,000	1 (5% convert from MT)	$5,000
Total			**$20,000**

As you can see, the volume of sales is a quarter of what was required before to hit the same targeted amount. With a higher conversion rate of low to mid and mid to high tickets, then the income target would further increase.

The idea is to move people from interest through to integration. Engaging with them along the way. Providing them with huge amounts of value and allowing for transformation to occur. This is what a successful experience ecosystem can provide.

SELLING SYSTEM

The fifth pillar of the Blue Ocean Formula is the selling system.

The selling system is focused on four key elements.

1. Connect.
2. Converse
3. Convert
4. Continue

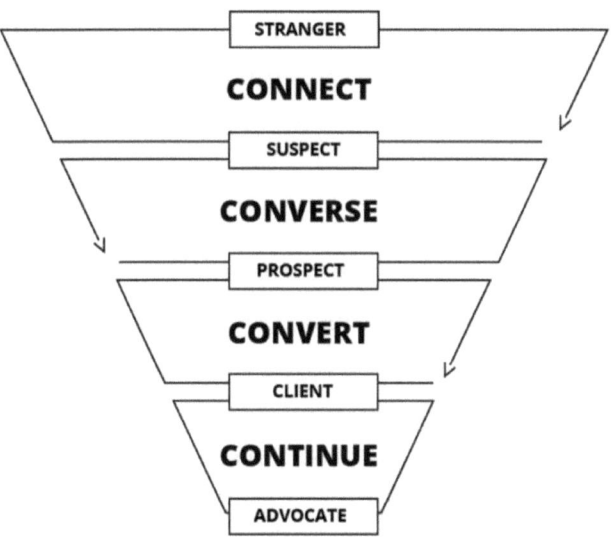

These four elements are key in getting people to know, like, and trust you. The know- like-trust factor is a marketing concept that states that people will do business with you if they know you, like you, and trust you. The goal is to get your strangers, suspects, prospects, and clients to understand and believe in you and the solution you provide.

Connect

If people don't know about you, your brand or your products then you will never sell anything. So the first part of the selling system is making connections with people in your target market. At this stage these people are strangers. You don't know who they are, and at this stage, they also don't know about you.

The purpose of the connect stage is to move them from strangers to suspects. They are someone who you suspect could benefit from, and be a fit for your program, but at this stage you still don't know much about them, including if they have a problem that you can solve.

Making connections
The best way to make connections is to put something of value in front of the stranger. Something that is going to attract their attention, something that is going to pique their interest (you can probably now see the linkage between the experience ecosystem and the sales system). Often, this is called a lead magnet.

You could do this in several ways, and it will depend on your market to test and see what works and resonates with them. Some of the value pieces that we have used and see working well with others in the marketing space include:

- **Free downloads** – eBooks, templates, checklists, and other file downloads have been a popular lead generation for businesses for many years. This could be an eBook that discusses the problems and solutions that your target market is having that align to the principles of your signature solution. For example, "The Five Ways to Make a Million Dollars in

30 Days". Alternatively, it could be a template or checklist that helps people move from problem to prize, but only giving enough to spark their interest.

- **Scorecards** - A scorecard is another great way to connect with your target market. A scorecard is a diagnostic tool (much like a quiz or questionnaire) that asks your target market a series of questions about their current situation or the problem they are facing. But it is not just about collecting answers from people. The scorecard provides instant valuable feedback to the person taking it, scoring them on how they are currently and providing valuable insights. It also provides you with great insights about your target market, making it a great win win.

- **Virtual events** - The chance to provide a sample of the education you offer can be a great way to attract the attention of potential clients. While this approach can be time-consuming, virtual events (aka webinars, workshops, masterclasses) are an excellent way to get to see and hear from you, building the connection. Handling webinars using systems like Zoom will enable you to get everyone involved and provide the opportunity for people to ask questions about your solution.

- **Mini-course** – The mini-course is another great way for people to hear from you (if a video mini-course) or get exposure to some of your educational content. The mini course could simply be a series of short videos on your learning platform. Alternatively, it could be a series of daily emails providing the information.

Organic vs paid

The first question to ask is where is my customer avatar spending their time online? Generally, this will be one of the various social media platforms. Probably Facebook, Instagram, or LinkedIn. But you may also find your prospects on other platforms such as YouTube, TikTok, Snapchat or Twitter. This information is critical to understanding your customer avatar. If you do not understand where your target audience is spending their time online or what kind of content they enjoy, you are not going to make the connections. It doesn't matter if you are using organic or paid posts –both are going to fail.

Once you know where they are, should you use organic or paid marketing? The simple answer is to do both and watch your analytics to see what is and isn't working. Making connections through organic posts is great, as it costs you nothing. But it can be a challenge. The algorithms are always changing and sometimes your organic posts may get a lot of engagement and other times not. Paid ads have the advantage of being able to be more targeted in putting your value content in front of strangers who fit your target. But do keep an eye on how your ads are performing and the return on your investment.

Converse

Ultimately, the goal of the connect stage is to engage people in a conversation. This is the critical piece. You need to engage people in a conversation so that you can tell them about:

- The problems you can solve.
- The value proposition your solution provides.
- The results they will get and the benefits of those results.
- The process that you follow to help them get the results.
- How you work with them and the investment they need to make.

But it is not just about telling them. Engaging them in a conversation also means that you can find out if they:

- Are really your target market.
- Have a problem you can solve.
- Will invest the time, money, and effort to get the results.
- Are the type of person who you want to work with.

This last point is important. By leveraging your expertise and having your sales system delivering you an ideal volume of clients means you do not have to work with everyone. You should be able to say no to certain people that you know will not be a good fit, or do not align to your values.

The conversation

The best sort of conversation is a one-to-one conversation, in person or virtually. Comes in the form of a discovery call where you ask questions and understand:

- Where they are now.
- Where they want to be.
- The challenges they are facing.
- If you can help them.

It is also a great opportunity to build on the know, like and trust factor that is so important in the sales process.

But connecting with a stranger that you provided some value content to and going straight to a discovery call will not be a frequent occurrence. Often you will need to converse with the prospect in other ways, such as:

- Replying to their comments on your social media posts.
- Sending direct email messages with more value content and a call-to-action.
- Connecting with them through text or messenger.

More recently, we are seeing (and hearing from others) that connecting through messenger is proving to be a much more successful process. With open rates of messages being much higher than the open rates of emails. I suspect this is because of the ease with which it is to open and respond to a text or message, combined with the overload of emails that we are getting daily.

Convert

The third stage in the sales system is the convert stage. Not everyone is going to get here, and the volume you get is going to depend on how well you connect and converse with the suspects and prospects. It is a sales funnel, and you will lose people along the way. Some just will not engage with you after accessing your value content, others will opt out along the way, and ideally you will also be able to filter out those that are not suitable or you don't want to work with.

This stage is about converting the prospects into clients. This is potentially after a discovery call, where the next step is for the prospect to join up to your program. However, depending on the solution and its cost, you may convert a prospect through email or messenger marketing (or even directly from an ad). The investment of the program is directly proportionate to the amount of conversation and the ease of converting.

Low ticket (interest or information) products will usually have a lower amount of touch points and you should look to convert directly from an offer in an ad, email or message. Higher ticket offers that require a higher investment will require a higher amount of conversation, both to satisfy the prospect's concerns but also to ensure they are the right fit for your program. Taking on clients that will not get the results, because they are not the right fit, is only going to result in more work and potentially damage your reputation.

Continue

The final stage is where we continue to add value to the client. Delivering an exceptional experience and converting them from clients to advocates.

Providing that huge amount of value, as we've taken them from stranger to suspect, to prospect, to client, will help to move them to become an advocate. They are connected with you. They are part of your community. And they then start advocating your services.

You want to constantly build on the know, like and trust factor. One of the best ways to do this is when someone else (that the stranger, suspect or prospect already knows, likes and trusts) advocates your services.

The continue stage also has another level. This is directly related to the experience ecosystem. You will have the initial conversion but depending where on the ecosystem the client is, there may be a further opportunity to convert them into a higher ticket program. Maybe they have purchased your initial information program, and are now on board with what you offer, and want to engage in your implementation or integration programs. Or maybe they have been through your implementation program but want to continue with you, accessing your knowledge and program and sign up for an ongoing membership program.

TECHNOLOGY & TOOLS

Now, even though this is the last pillar, this is one of the most critical pieces in the whole formula. It is the critical piece, because if we get this wrong, if we do not have the necessary technology and tools in place, people are not going to be able to engage with your experience ecosystem. You will not be able to move them through your selling system. They are not going to be able to consume the valuable content that you have created through your signature solution. But this pillar is last for a reason.

Often, what we see is people creating a learning experience and the first thing they will consider is the technology that they need. I don't know how many posts I have seen on Facebook with people asking, What is the best platform to use? It is the wrong approach!

The Learning Platform

Not every learning platform is the same. We have got Learning Management Systems (LMS), Learning Experience Platforms (LXP) as well as content aggregation systems that you can use to promote and sell your course. The run yourself LMS & LXP's come in a variety of types. There are the ones that are WordPress (and other content management system) based plugins. There are other ones that are better designed for the small course creator. Then there are others that were developed for large corporates. They all have a number of similarities (namely host a learning experience), but they also have their own specific functions and differ in several ways.

Selecting a platform that a large corporate would use and then trying to use that for the small course that you are delivering to an outside audience is either going to be overkill or is not going to work.

Starting with a technology first approach means that you may end up being very limited with the type of experience you can create.

I have had so many conversations with people about the types of learning experiences they want to create, and the platform that is best for each of them is different.

For example, one client wanted to have a strong community-based approach to the learning experience. The community was the focal point, with a social network of like-minded people that the client could also offer courses to. Another client wanted to engage learners using gamification principles (points and badges to reward and motivate engagement). Another client wanted to engage people with an app-based platform that they could deliver their courses through. And another client wanted to build a site that they could offer self-paced online courses, but also allow for some people to buy bundles of courses and others to access the courses through a membership program.

These clients required a completely different learning platform to deliver on their needs, and if they had approached the project with a technology first mindset, they would have failed in their desires.

Ok, so rant finished on the learning platform piece, but I know that this is an important but often missed point.

> If you are interested in finding out about some of the learning platforms in the market, you can jump onto our Academy (https://www.mavenzeal.academy/). We've got a free course there where we have done a lot of research into several different platforms. It is the Ultimate Guide to Learning Platforms. In this guide we provide a breakdown of the many course platforms helping edupreneurs get their expertise online.

Content creation tools

There is a wide range of content creation tools to have in your toolkit. This includes tools for creation of the learning assets and creation of content for marketing your programs. The exact tools you are going to use will depend on the learning experiences you are going to create, and the type of learning platform, but generally you would be looking at video creation and editing tools, presentation development tools, interactive eLearning tools, and tools to create worksheets and templates.

Other content creation tools to consider include:

- Animation tools to create animated videos, explainer videos and edumercials.
- Content writing tools to assist with the grammar and proofreading of your content.
- Image creation tools for the creation of images to be included in courses, presentations, webinars, blog posts and social media marketing.
- Image mock-up tools used to create images of screenshots and products in real-world environments.

Customer relationship management database (CRM)

Another critical piece in the technology stack is your Customer Relationship Management Database (CRM). As we move people through the selling system, we need to capture their details and track where they are in the process. We also need the CRM to act as an autoresponder. A tool that is going to be able to send out emails to those people as part of your converse process.

As with learning platforms, there is a plethora of CRMs in the market and it's also important to consider the:

- Functions it provides.
- Cost to use.
- Ability to integrate with other technology and tools, such as the learning platform.

Landing pages

Landing pages are designed to promote your offer. They differ from a website as they are focused on the single offer. In most cases, you should have a landing page builder either with your CRM or learning platform, but you may choose to use another standalone landing page builder that might have some additional features you want (such as upsell and down sell sequences).

If you go with a standalone landing page builder, then consider how that will integrate with your learning platform and CRM. Also consider if it will be able to collect payment through a payment provider like Stripe or PayPal.

Automation tools

The last piece to look at is the automation tools. You want to have a CRM that will create an automation that when a certain event happens, it will trigger another event. For example, someone signs up for an eBook and they are then automatically emailed with a link to the eBook. And after a couple of days, then they receive another email as part of your converse sequence.

Also, think about all the other potential automation tools that are going to take away your time. Ideally, you don't want to be doing all the manual work with the technology as that will consume so much of your time. You want to be in an 80/20 position. Where 80% of the tasks that are happening as part of the technology are happening automatically. There is probably going to be about 20% of tasks that cannot be automated because you need to provide that personalised service.

So, you've got a whole range of different tools and technologies to consider to create and deploy your ecosystem of experiences. Also, the tools to provide that selling system, so lots of technology to consider. But if you've gone through the process and you have put all the other pillars in place, it is going to become a lot easier because you will have a clear idea on exactly what your ecosystem experience will be. You have a clear idea on what your selling system will be. And that really narrows down the tools and tech that you are going to need.

PART 4

THE 7 STEPS TO THE BLUE OCEAN

Leveraging your expertise to move into the blue ocean involves transforming what you know into an ecosystem of experiences. It involves creating a digital learning experience.

When creating a new learning experience, there are often several common mistakes that are made. These mistakes can have a negative impact on the learning experience.

Based on 20 years of learning design experience, where I have developed thousands of hours of learning content, across many industries and organisation types, I have developed a proven seven step process to leverage your expertise and avoid these mistakes.

This seven-step process will take you from having the knowledge stuck in your head, to having a course with students enrolled and engaged in.

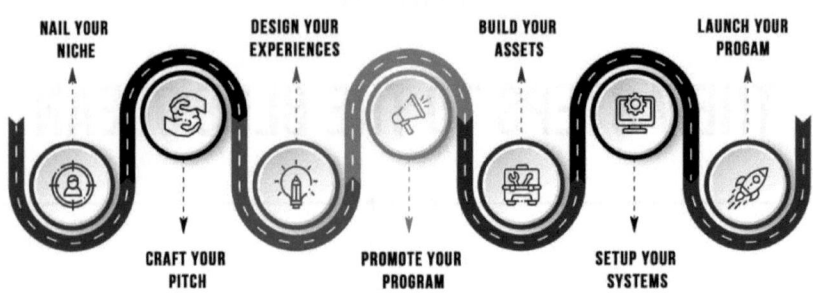

STEP 1 — NAIL YOUR NICHE

The first stage in the design process is to define the niche market you are targeting and understanding the problem you can solve.

It is getting clear about where you want to be going and what that looks like. Without having this clear vision of the destination, we often see coaches, consultants and aspiring course creators wasting time with unnecessary development, going around in circles, or worse, getting stuck in analysis paralysis. In addition, we see the wrong types of courses being developed because the desired end state and the course type do not align.

This step is also about defining the destination for your target market. This is where you nail your niche and understand the problems the target market is having so you can define a solution, that will take your ideal client from problem to prize.

THE 7 STEPS TO THE BLUE OCEAN

To define the destination, we explore the following five sub steps of:

1. Purpose
2. Position
3. Persona
4. Pains
5. Prize

PURPOSE

The purpose of the learning experience ties back into the experience ecosystem and understanding what the learning experience looks like.

Creating a learning experience aimed at generating interest in the course would be very knowledge based, making the participant aware of the solution. It would usually be self-directed and require little (if any) facilitation effort from yourself. This type of learning experience could be delivered to many.

An information only experience would be very knowledge based. Educating participants on the core concepts, providing information they need to undertake the desired performance outcomes. The information course would usually be self-directed and may require little facilitation effort from yourself. This type of learning experience could be delivered to many.

An implementation experience is aimed at the application of the acquired knowledge to complete a task. For this to occur, the participants are going to need more support and therefore your level of participation will be much greater. As a result, numbers of participants will be less.

An integration learning experience goes beyond implementation. It is where you are looking at developing mastery. This learning experience cannot be simply solved by providing an online course. It involves a high degree of facilitation, coaching and support and is often delivered to a much smaller cohort of learners, if not one-on-one.

POSITION

Position is about the position you want to take in the niche. Are you going to be very generalised across the niche or are you going to be more targeted and position yourself within a sub niche. It is also worth deciding if you are going to be positioning yourself as a premium product or a lower cost product. Part of this positioning will also depend on the type of course or program you are offering.

What Type of Course

Part of determining the learning experience involves determining the type of course that you are going to deliver. Essentially, there are four types of courses to create.

Mini-course

A mini-course, as the name suggests, is a short course designed to be completed in a couple of hours. With mini-courses, size doesn't matter as each one provides insight into a particular topic in a digestible way or provides a gateway for more in-depth learning on a subject.

The great thing about mini-courses is that they can be repurposed from wider topics or created to focus on a particular area. Many people who create online courses use them to draw in users to register for a longer course, as well as use them as add-ons for a particular subject.

A mini-course is also a great way to test the market for interest in a larger course you are making. With a mini-course, you can see interest in your topic before investing your time and resources into a much more extensive course. If your audience buys your mini-course, that means that you have evidence that your larger course will sell.

Massive Open Online Courses (MOOC)

A Massive Open Online Course, also known as a MOOC, is generally a self-paced online course designed to help people learn a new skill or increase their knowledge. In addition, this course could include a community for learners to interact and may have facilitation by you as the expert.

Using a range of tools and content types, including text and presentations, video, animation, discussions, etc., MOOC style courses provide an engaging way for learners to develop the knowledge and skills they need.

Masterclass

A masterclass is a signature course, designed to share the expert's knowledge with people who want to know about it. This type of course is usually a combination of self-paced online resources, combined with virtual facilitated discussions with the expert. Learners may also have regular one-to-one sessions from the master trainer.

As an opportunity to 'learn from the best', a masterclass should include a unique type of content and insight that people can't get anywhere else.

Membership Site

Membership sites provide access to an ongoing selection of exclusive content for members. Membership sites can provide a range of online courses designed to enhance knowledge of a subject, which sometimes sits alongside other content such as articles, whitepapers, and access to different templates and tools.

Membership sites require ongoing development of learning assets to ensure that new content is provided to members, so membership subscriptions are renewed.

These four course types align with the ecosystem funnel. A mini course would be around generating interest, possibly touching on providing information. A MOOC would be around providing information. The masterclass and membership sites would be designed to provide implementation or integration.

PERSONA

When defining the destination, it is important to have user understanding. Without a clear idea of who is going to be accessing the content, how can you deliver an effective learning experience? You need a clear understanding of the user persona – who they are, their needs, goals, motivations and frustrations and design content that is going to be of benefit to those users.

Often, I see learning materials, and courses being created without user experience in mind. As a result, the levels of engagement and the retention of information falls. The experience doesn't have as much positive impact. So, it is critical to clearly understand who your users are to craft a learning experience that fits. It will also help when you look at generating desire in your course.

User understanding is also about providing relevant and contextual content. Relevance is needed for both engagement and in the retention of the information. People remember stories not facts. By building context into the course through the use of stories, people will retain the information easier. If people cannot see relevance in what they are doing, then they are going to struggle to apply that knowledge later. People will be engaged as well when they can see the WIIFM What's in it For Me. And they get this, through context.

The PERSONAS model

So, what do we look at? To make this process easier, I have developed the PERSONAS Model, to provide a framework to look at the elements that are required for user understanding.

This includes looking at a basic profile, developing empathy for the user, exploring their reasons (or motivations), their skills, knowledge and experiences, obstacles to learning, their needs, and how they access technology.

In the persona development process, you are not trying to capture the key characteristics of every possible user. Rather, two or three key stereotypical personas of people that you are going to be working with. You may also develop two or three personas as part of the process.

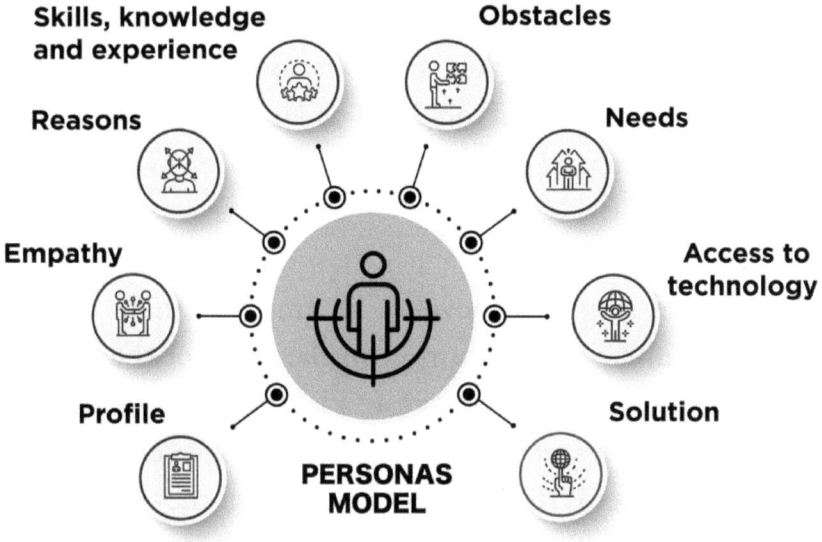

Profile

The first step in the PERSONAS Model is developing a profile for that persona. This starts with looking at the general age range of that persona group. Now, while I don't believe in designing for generational differences, there are still certain differing characteristics between younger and older people. Generally, this would be around the life experiences that they would have had, which can impact on their learning process and the information they need.

- What is their gender, occupation, family, and location?
- Are the users predominantly male or female?
- Are they in management or a business owner?
- Do they have family (and what experiences might they have had related to this)?

- Are they located in your local area, in your country or overseas? If they are overseas, what impact does this have on factors such as language and literacy and internet capabilities?

Empathy

The second step is to develop an empathy map. This is an opportunity to put yourself in the shoes of the user. It provides an opportunity to create a learning experience that meets the learner where they are at. It involves considering what the learner is thinking or feeling, what they are seeing, hearing, and doing.

Often, we see at this point that multiple personas get created. One cohort may be feeling nervous or apprehensive, while another may be feeling excited. As a result, the experiences we develop may vary and further elements of the PERSONAS model may be different based on the empathy map.

Reasons

The third part of the persona model is looking at the reason. What is the reason for people actually engaging in your course? What is the problem that you are solving for them? What are their motivations for wanting to do your course? If you cannot understand what their motivations are, you are going to find it very hard to design an experience that is going to tap into that.

Also, think about what their goals are. What are they hoping to achieve? Again, if you are designing and delivering a learning experience that is not aligned to those goals, you are going to have some issues around the design and delivery of that program.

Skills, knowledge, and experience
The next part is looking at their skills, knowledge, and experience. A key adult learning principle is that adults bring life experiences and knowledge to a program. You need to consider these experiences to allow the learners to connect their experiences with current knowledge and activities. Consider how you will relate the learner's previous experiences to the current learning experience.

Understanding the audience's skills, knowledge, and experiences provides a benchmark for delivery of the content. Without considering this aspect you run the risk of delivering content that is too high level and confusing which can lose your learners. Alternatively, you may deliver the learning at too low a level and demotivate your learners.

It is also an opportunity to consider what the learner's ideal learning experience is and considering how this aligns with what you have developed as part of your strategy.

Obstacles
The fifth step in the model is to consider the obstacles or challenges that your learners face.

What obstacles they are facing? What are the barriers to change? How can you overcome these barriers? What are the frustrations that they may have? What are their frustrations in what they are doing?

Also, consider any roadblocks that they may have towards learning. This could be related to language or literacy. It could also be because of preconceived notions and wrong thinking.

Needs
Step six explores the learners' needs. This includes both the rational and emotional needs.

As much as we might want to believe most of our decisions and actions are rational, the reality is that they are emotionally driven by our lizard brain. The lizard brain controls our subconscious and research suggests that over 95% of our behaviour is subconscious. For this reason, we need to trigger emotions to change behaviour. Therefore, we need to consider the emotional and rational needs of our persona in designing the learning experience.

Access to technology
Next, consider how learners access technology. This involves four key questions:

1. How do they most commonly access information? Via desktop, laptop or mobile device?

2. What is their preferred method of communication? Email, phone, Skype, WhatsApp, text or in-person?
3. Where are they social? An important question to consider if trying to build an online community. Is it Facebook, LinkedIn, Twitter, Instagram or some other social media channel?
4. What is their proficiency level with technology?

Solution

The final step to be taken is when you develop the solution and create the learning experience. At this time, you need to revisit the persona you have created and consider it against the solution that you have created.

Key questions to ask:

1. How does the problem you solve relate to their goals?
2. How does the solution connect with their needs (both rational and emotional)?
3. How does the solution build on their skills/knowledge/experience?
4. How does the solution connect with their access to technology?

PROBLEM

The end goal of any learning experience should be to solve a problem. Remember that people don't want to buy your course. They want to buy the solution that your course provides. They want a solution to the problem they have. They want something that takes their pain away. This is what you need to get clear at this stage. What is the solution you provide that addresses their pain points?

Are you creating vitamin or painkiller courses?

What are vitamin courses? Vitamins can be described as nice to have, and not need to have. Just as people take vitamins to improve their health, a vitamin course is one that someone takes to improve themselves.

These can be great courses. They can provide much needed information and help people to gain valuable knowledge, skills and improved performance. However, they are not the courses that generate a huge desire. They are not the courses that attract huge enrolments, and often they are not the courses with high completion rates.

When statistics are provided on the low completion rates of online courses, I believe that many of these are vitamin courses. Just like the numerous containers of unfinished and expired vitamins many of us have laying around (I have a cupboard filling up with them) many learners also have a collection of unfinished vitamin courses. They had great intentions of taking them but because it was not a need to have or because other distractions occurred the course was left on the digital shelf, unfinished.

What is a painkiller course? As the name suggests, a painkiller course addresses the individuals pain points. As opposed to the vitamin course that is nice to have a painkiller course is a must have. As a result, it is a course that people will desire.

The painkiller course addresses an immediate and unmet need. It is something your learners will want. Something they will consume readily. Something that they will be willing to pay for if it solves their pain.

The painkiller course also often has a shorter sales cycle. They are in pain, and they want the pain to be taken away as quickly as possible. If your course clearly explains how it solves their pain, then you are going to find it much easier to sell. You may not have to put much effort into selling the course to them.

If the course you are creating is a vitamin course, perhaps you should consider shifting to creating a painkiller course to increase the enrolments and engagement in your courses. Both types must be well developed and well delivered courses, but a painkiller course is something that your learners are going to desire more.

Avoiding the kitchen sink syndrome

One of the big mistakes that I see when people are building their online course is this problem that I call the kitchen sink syndrome.

This occurs when course creators think that they must provide the learners with a heap of content. The result is this huge course full of information that overwhelms the learners.

When too much information is provided, learners suffer from cognitive overload. They end up not remembering the key points that we need them to remember. We also find that they disengage. Brain-based study has shown that physiologically, your neurons are keen and alert for only 20 consecutive minutes. At the end of those 20 minutes, your neurons have gone from full-fledged alert to total collapse. Delivering less content eliminates cognitive overload.

When you focus on delivering a solution to solve a specific problem, the content you provide is more succinct, it doesn't overwhelm and allows you to really hit the target for those learners.

Validating your idea

One of the best ways to identify the problems and be really clear about how your solution aligns to the persona is to conduct some market research. It is possible that you've made some wrong assumptions about your audience, who they are and what they feel are the major pain points for them. Market research will allow you to get further clarity about what they need and are feeling. It also gives you the opportunity to learn about how they talk about their problems and pains, so you can craft your message in their language.

Only by doing market research can you tell whether your course is likely to be a success. Market research could also help you find faults in your current course model and help you make improvements before the official launch.

Surveys

One of the best forms of market research is surveys. You can use surveys to get an idea of who your audience is, as well as finding out what they look for in a course. If your course is on a very niche topic, surveys could be important for establishing whether there is a market out there at all. You may also want to target people individually through emails or by visiting them in person.

Keyword search

You could also use a keyword search tool to see how many people are looking for words related to your course. This will give you an indication as to whether people are looking for the course you provide, but also the actual keywords they are using (which will help with marketing your course later on). You can also see the click potential of the keywords, which will help to identify any competitors.

Research your competitors

Researching competitors' courses could be very important for borrowing ideas and for contrastingly setting yourself apart. Look at the outline offered by other courses and read reviews of other courses to get an idea of what is out there. You may even be able to survey people who have taken these other courses to see what they think they would change. Certain course subjects are likely to be more competitive than others, in which cases you may have to do more thorough research.

Social media

Viewing conversations on social media and forum sites also provides an insight into what learners are saying, how they are expressing themselves and what solutions they may have already tried to remedy their pains.

PRIZE

The last part in defining the destination is to define the prize. People are going to pay for the prize that solves their problem. And the more compelling you can make the prize, then the easier it will be to promote and attract clients.

The prize is your value proposition. It is how you are going to make life better for your client. And you need to make sure that your value proposition comes with a strong emotional hook.

As much as we like to tell ourselves that our decisions are rational and based on logic, more than 90% of our decisions are emotional. A strong emotional hook that ties into what the client is feeling and how they could feel once they undertake your program is going to make it much better to engage your target market.

Consider the following:

"How to get started with Facebook ads"

"Discover how to use Facebook ads to get more leads and make more sales"

Which one has the better prize? Which one taps into the emotions more? The second one, right?

The first one tells you that you are going to learn about Facebook ads, but is that really the problem they are facing? You could assume that they want to run Facebook ads for a reason – probably to get more leads and make more sales.

Think about the pain point that your audience faces and the single solution that you are offering.

GET CLARITY ON THE PROBLEM AND PRIZE

I can't stress enough how critical this part is in the learning design process. If you do not clearly understand the problem you are solving and the pain points you need to address, then you will not be clear on the solution.

If you are not clear on the solution, then you cannot articulate the desired performance outcomes. It is critically important, as part of any sort of learning experience to have a clear understanding of the performance outcomes. It is about what we want people to do at the end of the learning. It is understanding the end goal.

If you don't have an understanding of the end goal, the desired performance outcomes, then you cannot create the appropriate learning journey to move people from where they are to where they need to be.

If you don't have an appropriate learning journey, the course structure will be off. You may struggle to engage the learners and they may not be motivated to complete the course if they cannot see what is in it for them.

You should not progress any further with your course development until you understand the problem and how your course delivers the required solution.

Questions to consider:

- What are the pain points you are addressing?
- What is the solution?
- What does a successful outcome look like?

STEP 2 - CRAFT YOUR PITCH

This second step is the critical piece that sets the foundation for the remainder of the steps. If you get this right, then the rest of the course development process becomes easy. Unfortunately, it is the one area that we see so many coaches, consultants and course creators struggle with. This delays the course development, or they just get it so wrong that the planned program doesn't deliver on the desired outcomes.

This is the exciting part that I love, where I work with my clients to extract that invaluable (but intangible) intellectual property in their head. In doing so we can create some valuable visual models that will make the rest of the learning design process easy. You will also have some great tools to help with the pitch and promotion of your program.

Before we move further in the process, it is worth explaining how we use the extremely powerful Think RAPT® system to get really clear about your intellectual property and your unique methodology. By getting this right, we fast-track the steps that follow.

Renée Hasseldine, CEO & Founder of Think RAPT®, explains the system in the extract on the following pages.

LEVERAGE YOUR EXPERTISE

THE THINK RAPT® SYSTEM

There are four types of visual model that we need for a complete set and we've got the acronym RAPT to remember these four models in the order we extract and present them.

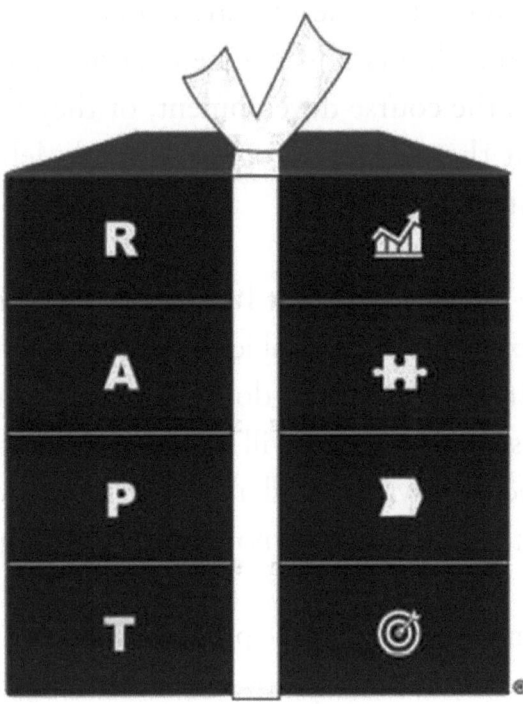

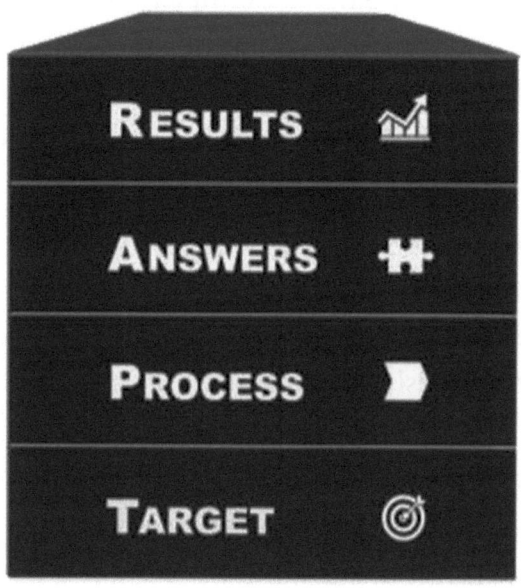

RESULTS MODEL

The first model is the Results Model. The Results Model allows the audience to identify the current results they are getting, the results that they want, and the gap between the two. When they see that there's a gap between where they are and where they want to be, they're going to be motivated to do something about it.

We want to use evocative emotive language in a Results Model. We want to be telling a story in a way that really captivates the audience's attention and inspires them into taking some action.

In addition to evocative and emotive language, we can also use icons to represent key performance indicators (KPIs) in your Results Model. Say for example, your audience really cares about how much income they're making, then you might use dollar signs to show how much income they make at each level in the Results Model as you present it.

ANSWERS MODEL

The ANSWERS MODEL demonstrates the answers to your audience's challenges. It outlines what they NEED in order to achieve their desired results.

The sweet spot for an Answers Model is between three and seven elements. More than seven can feel unwieldy. Less than three will feel unsubstantial.

An Answers Model contains nouns, because these are the things that your audience needs to be successful.

The icons in an Answers Model are for aesthetic purposes. It's not like with the Results Model where the icons usually represent KPIs. Appropriate Answers Model shapes are nonlinear. We want something that looks like parts of a whole.

Some possible metaphors are:

- the things you need in your suitcase
- the pieces of the puzzle.

PROCESS MODEL

The PROCESS MODEL outlines your proven methodology, your unique way of getting your clients from A to B. It outlines your unique process for delivering results for your clients. It is the basis of your service delivery. The Process Model is all about ACTION. The things that need to be done. So make sure you use verbs. And just like in the Answers Model, the icons in a Process Model are there for aesthetic purposes.

The sweet spot for a Process Model is between three to seven steps.

A Process Model should be linear. There may be some tiny exceptions to this rule, but there's a really important reason behind the linear shape for a Process Model. Have you ever been in a taxi in a foreign city and wondered if your driver was taking you the 'long way' or 'round and round in circles'? You DO NOT want your clients to feel like that is happening with your solutions.

Remember, the Process Model is showing your audience how you're going to get them out of the pain that they're in.

If they're in enough pain that they're willing to pay you for a solution, then they want to get out of that pain as fast as possible.

The shortest distance between two points is a straight line.

A circular shape for a Process Model feels like you're going round and round in circles inside the pain. That's not going to be easy to sell!

Use a linear shape for your Process Model to reassure your audience that you will get them out of their pain ASAP!

TARGET MODEL

The TARGET MODEL highlights the benefits or KPIs that your solution is targeting. It shows your clients what they 'get' and answers the important 'What's in it for me?' question. As per the Answers and Process Models, the icons in a Target Model are for aesthetics.

The ideal number of benefits in a Target Model is three. This is something that we have learned over time, with years of experience creating these models for clients.

What we've found is, if you have a Target Model with six benefits in it, by the time you get to it in your presentation, it starts to feel awkward. It feels like you're going on and on and on and throwing in a set of steak knives.

Three elements in a Target Model works best in terms of the rhythm of a presentation.

You get this, this and this. Boom. Drop the mic.

Short, sharp and punchy. Appropriate Target Model shapes are nonlinear. We want something that looks like parts of a whole.

If your audience is individuals, the benefits they are interested in are generally some variation or form of the following:

- Certainty
- Variety
- Significance
- Love/Connection
- Growth
- Contribution
- Clarity
- Relationships
- Purpose
- Results
- Passion
- Fun

If your audience is businesses, if you're B2B, the benefits they are interested in are generally some variation or form of the following:

- Time
- Money
- Stress
- Legacy
- Clients

- Leads
- Profile

Make sure you do your market research and use your audience's own words and language to label the benefits.

ANSWERING WHY, WHAT AND HOW

Each model in the Think RAPT® system fulfils a different role, but they are most POWERFUL when used together.

- The Results and Target Models are about WHY your clients should work with you.
- The Answers Model is about WHAT they need to succeed.
- The Process Model is about HOW you get results.

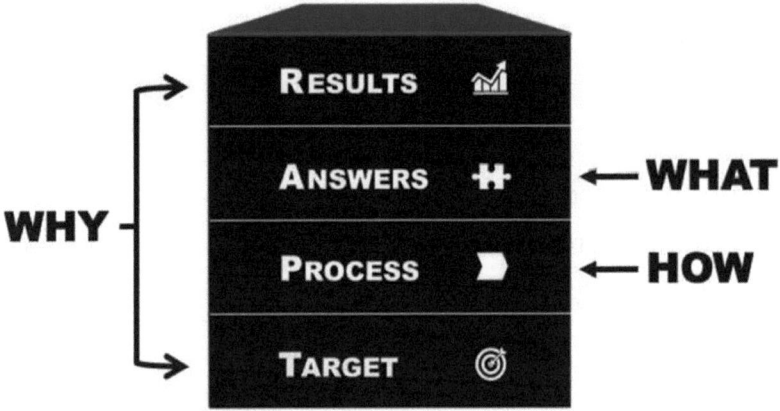

THE EMOTIONAL RATIONAL SANDWICH

When used together, the four models create an emotional-rational sandwich, that helps your ideal client say 'hell yes' to your solution.

The Results Model and the Target Model are the emotional bread. The Answers Model and the Process model are the rational filling.

By using all four models together, you answer both the emotional and rational needs of your audience in their decision-making process. People make decisions based on how they feel and they justify them with logic. By using all four models, you give your audience all the information they need to make an informed decision.

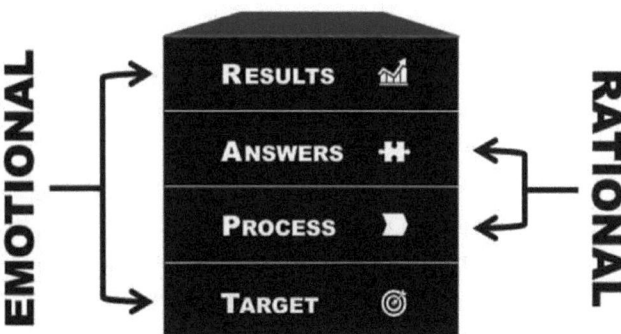

Unpacking your intellectual property into these visual models provides the foundation for the learning experience design. The Process Model gives us the framework for the learning experience. It outlines each of the steps needed to move the learner from problem to prize.

With this part of the ecosystem mapped out, we can then delve deeper into each of the steps to determine what is needed to achieve that step. Effectively, we are creating some more visual models for each step, so we can outline the behaviours and actions required to achieve that step.

For example, in our process model, the first step is to define the destination and under that step we explore the following four sub steps of:

1. Purpose
2. Persona
3. Problem
4. Prize

You would complete this process for each step, so you have defined sub-steps for each.

The process of unpacking the visual models also provides you with the framework for the entire ecosystem, where you can map out the interest, information, implementation, and integration products.

STEP 3 - DESIGN YOUR EXPERIENCES

The third step is where we design the detail. Where the learning experience design really kicks in. Where we explore the learner's journey and develop the experiences, we want them to have. So often we see course creators getting this step wrong. After having developed a structure for their experience, they then follow some bad advice and simply create a series of video recordings not considering any other type of learning experience that may provide better learning outcomes or engage the user in a better way.

Do not underestimate the importance of good design in providing a positive learning experience. If the learning experience is not positive, learners will disengage. A disengaged learner will not focus on the content, will not retain the information, and therefore will not achieve the desired outcomes. So, creating this positive experience and delivering the content in several ways is an important part.

It is at this step that we utilise our 4P content design model, where we design how we can:

- **Provoke** interest or attention in the topic.
- **Provide** the context and content.
- Create opportunities to **practice.**
- Create a framework to assist the learner to **perform.**

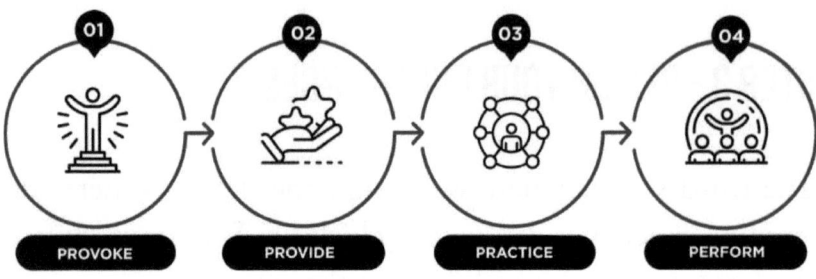

PROVOKE

To get people engaged in your learning content, you need to switch their brain on. You need to capture their attention and let them see the clear benefits. To do this you want to create an eye-catching headline, fact, or statistic that will get their attention.

Develop some questions for participants to reflect on the problem and how it impacts them, or how their previous experiences relate to the problem.

Another way to provoke the learner is to provide a story that is going to engage them, that will activate their brain.

The power of stories

Once upon a time… stories were told to entertain, educate, and engage. Storytelling has been around as long as civilization has existed. Stories in sacred text thousands of years old have withstood the test of time and are still told across the world today. You will remember a parable told to you as a child yet struggle to remember what you did at work on Monday. The way stories are told has changed. Instead of gathering around a campfire, we play role play video games, follow celebrities on social media or watch movies and TV shows. The one thing that hasn't changed is the power of a good story.

Stories give meaning to the otherwise meaningless. Stories provide an effective way to engage learners with the content. A good story provides some context around the topic, to provide some characters that people can relate to.

When we undertake training that uses boring bullet points or text, our language processing part of the brain is activated. This part decodes the words into meaning, but nothing else happens. When told a story, it is not only the language parts of the brain that are activated. Other areas of the brain that are used to experience the events of the story are switched on. Our whole brain is put to work.

Stories provide an immersive learning experience. They make learning more memorable and fun. People always remember a good story. Therefore, they will have a higher retention of the content covered in the learning.

PROVIDE

The next step is to provide the information. This starts by providing a big picture overview.

Some people are big picture people and need to see the big picture first before drilling down into the details. Other people are detail-oriented and want to be given the finer details. They rarely need to see the big picture but giving them the big picture before getting into the details is not a huge issue. They might be keen to get into the details, but overall, it will not be a bad experience. On the other hand, if you jumped straight into the details the big picture people are going to be lost. They will struggle with the details as they don't have the big picture to see where everything fits. It is going to be a difficult learning experience and will impact them a lot more negatively than giving the big picture to the detail-oriented people.

Provide a big picture overview. This could be an image, model or metaphor that connects everything together. Then put the big picture into context. Here, provide an outline of the benefits and what happens if the learner doesn't follow or misses this step. Adding the context is going to provide the relevance. People need to have some relevance, they need to see where the content is relevant to them. The only way they can do that is if there is some context around the materials.

Relevance is needed for both engagement and the retention of the information. By building context into the course, people will retain the information easier. If people cannot see relevance in what they are doing, then they are going to struggle to apply that knowledge later. People will be more engaged when they can see the What's in it For Me (WIIFM). They get this through context.

Then you want to provide the content. But not too much content. Research done into the brain and memory suggests that we only have so much information that we can retain in our brain. There is a myth that we have an attention span shorter than a goldfish. While this is incorrect, we do have a limit of how much information we can retain. Miller's Information Processing Theory states that the short-term memory can only hold five to nine chunks of information. So, list the five to nine key points of content needed for participants to complete the activities and perform the actions.

Then provide guidance on how participants can apply the knowledge.

PRACTICE

The third step in the model is to outline the action steps or activities participants need to apply their skills and knowledge.

If we look at any learning that is done, it is done with a goal of doing something. We are learning something to do something. There is a performance element to it. So, you need to create some activities or opportunities for the participants to practice what they have been learning.

If you are just providing an information course, then you may not get to this step. But when providing an implementation course, the opportunity to practice the performance required is crucial.

PERFORM

The final step is to provide a metric for participants to assess themselves. Alternatively, develop some questions that they can use to reflect on how well they performed in the practice. Also consider any opportunity to give feedback on progress and performance.

Then detail the next steps to allow them to improve and integrate.

STEP 4 – PROMOTE YOUR PROGRAM

The fourth step is creating desire for the learning experience. This is about developing a marketing campaign that will generate interest and sales before we start the asset creation process.

Determining desire before we have undertaken the heavy lifting of building the assets for the learning course will overcome the build it and they will come mistake that many course creators make. Just because you have built a course doesn't mean that people are going to find it and enroll in it.

RAISE THEIR HAND

The best way you can determine desire in your course or program, is to get people to show that they are interested. You want them to raise their (probably virtual) hand as an expression of interest.

This is where you want to engage with your audience on social media, email people on your list, and talk to potential, current, and previous clients. Tell your audience about the prize that your program delivers and find out if people would be interested if it was made available.

If people are raising their hand and saying yes, they are interested then you have been able to determine desire in your program.

PRESELL YOUR PROGRAM

Once you engage potential customers, take the opportunity to presell your program. The best way to determine desire in your program is to get people to reach into their pockets and pay for your program. There is no better determination of desire than putting money down.

You might feel uncomfortable about preselling before you have even started building, but it is a very common practice (not just with online courses), and you should not feel anxious or uncomfortable about doing so.

Preselling provides you with the benefit of being able to determine desire. It also provides you with the funds to pay for the building of the assets. Potentially, you could presell enough seats in your program to pay for the upcoming development costs. However, you would generally offer the presold program at a discount or offer additional features to encourage people to buy into your program well before the launch.

Before preselling, set a goal on the number of enrolments you want to get before starting to build. If you don't get these numbers, you can then consider if there is enough desire and if you will continue with building the program or else make adjustments to increase desire. If your minimum numbers are not met you may choose to refund the people who pre-purchased, explaining that there was not enough interest in the program.

A word of warning

If you are going to presell, then you need to be committed to delivering on the program. Generally, you would look at preselling less than eight weeks before (more likely four-six weeks) the program launch and if you are not confident in hitting the goal of having the program completed in that time then I would recommend you reconsider doing a presell campaign. If you are prone to procrastination, distraction or not hitting your goals then preselling might not be for you.

DELIVERING A LIVE MINIMAL VIABLE PRODUCT (MVP)

An alternative to doing a presell is delivering the first version of your program as a live MVP. If you have followed the process to this point, you will have designed the detail to take your clients from problem to prize and can deliver this as a live virtual program.

In the live virtual program, you would deliver all the content via Zoom, Teams, or whatever virtual tool you prefer. There would be minimal development involved with the creation of a presentation, and some worksheets or templates.

Not only does the live MVP give you the benefit of determining desire and generating some immediate income, but it also gives you the ideal opportunity to test your program. In the live MVP you get to hear all the questions that your audience has and find any gaps in your program.

USING THE PRICE MODEL TO DETERMINE YOUR SELLING PRICE

One of the common questions I often get asked when people are building online courses is -*What price do I sell my course for?* Unfortunately, there is no magic formula or simple one size fits all solution. There are a number of factors to consider when pricing your course.

These factors outlined in our PRICE model look at:

- Profit
- Results
- Involvement
- Course Length
- Expertise

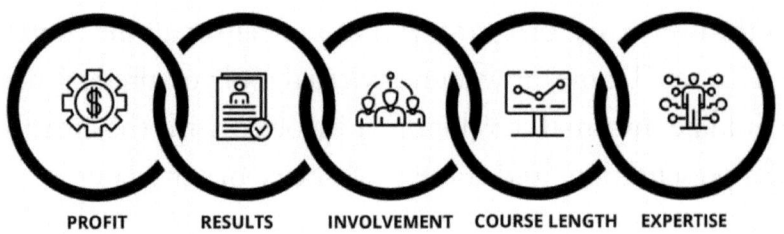

Profit

The first factor to consider is profit. This is about starting with the end in mind. Starting with an idea of the profit that you want to achieve and working backwards from there.

So, step one is to understand your profit target. The period for your profit target could be anything - a day, a month, a quarter, or a year. The period doesn't matter as the calculations we do remain the same.

For example, if you have a profit target of $12,000 and a proposed price of $1,000 for your program, then 12 sales are required to reach the profit target.

It is at this point it's important to define your metrics. Now 12 sales might not sound too daunting (and it might not be), but you need to understand two key metrics. They are the:

1. Sales to leads conversion ratio – this is the number of leads that you need to put your offer in front of to get the desired sales.
2. Leads to reach conversion ration – the number of people you need to reach to generate the required volume of leads.

For example, if your sales to leads ratio is one percent and your leads to reach conversion ratio is ten percent then you would need to generate 1200 leads to hit the 12 sales required, which would mean you need to reach 12,000 people.

So now you can consider the realities of this price, the number of enrolments and, subsequently, the leads you need to generate. This is the point where you can then revise the course price, based on the ease or difficulty of the leads and reach required.

Now if you're new, and you haven't sold a course before, then you may not really have a good grasp on the metrics so I would use the data we have provided in the table below.

Price	Sales to Leads Conversion %
$1 - $99	2.50%
$100 - $999	1.50%
$1,000 - $1,999	1.00%
$2,000 +	0.50%

Table 1 - Average conversion metrics for selling courses

Results

The second factor to consider is the results. What are the results that your learning program is going to deliver for the participants? What is the value of those results?

If it's just a simple set and forget information delivery course, then it probably doesn't provide a huge amount of value. But if you have a course and people are implementing what you are telling them to do, consider the impact of that knowledge that you are sharing. Consider if you are providing ten times return value on the cost price.

For example, is your $1,000 course going to help people generate $10,000 in sales or savings?

With the value, consider everything that you are bundling into the package. The course, coaching, virtual events, tools and templates. A bigger course package, can provide more value and can command a higher price.

Involvement

The third factor to consider is your involvement. If you are just building a simple set and forget course, where people enrol, go through the course at their own pace, and have little involvement in it, then you are probably going to sell at a lower price. Alternatively, if your course is going to require a large amount of your time (for example weekly coaching sessions, individual coaching sessions, being engaged in discussions, being available for questioning and commenting) then you would factor in the cost of your time into the course as part of that value.

Course length

The fourth factor in the price model is to consider the length of the course. A short course length equates to low dollars, while a long course length equals higher dollars. You are also going to find that a larger course length, something that's spaced out over time, is going to give more people opportunities to implement or integrate, which will provide more value and is probably going to have you more involved.

Expertise

The fifth factor to consider is your expertise and the perception around you as the expert. If we look at branding of cars, such as BMW against Kia. BMW is perceived as being a higher quality car. Therefore, they are charging more for the price. The same with people. Are you perceived as a person of influence, someone who is an expert in your industry? If you are, then you could charge more based on your reputation.

STEP 5 - BUILD YOUR ASSETS

Knowing that we have tested our idea and generated sufficient desire, the fifth step is to start building the assets for the course. This is certainly one of the largest and most time-consuming pieces of the creation process, but if you have done the earlier steps well and conducted a thorough scoping and analysis you should be developing quality assets that are going to deliver a superb learning experience.

SELECTING THE ASSETS TO BUILD

Depending on the type of learning experience you are creating, there could be a variety of assets that you will need or want to build for your program.

These include:

- Video assets.
- Interactive eLearning assets.
- Visual assets.
- Presentation assets.
- Supplementary assets.

Video assets

Video has always been an extremely powerful tool for delivering learning, offering a way to convey information in an engaging way. In the past, producing videos for yourself was too expensive and time-consuming, but this has changed in recent years. We now have access to the tools and technologies to create a range of videos.

Talking head presentations

Talking head presentation videos work exactly how their name suggests. The presenter appears on screen as a talking head, sometimes accompanied with information and graphics in the background. This type of video makes it easy to provide both verbal and graphical information, while also being easier to produce than some other methods.

Screencast

Screencast or slide share videos work by providing you with something to talk about. Each slide or screen will enable you to talk and provide information to your learners, while also providing them with video steps to make it easier for them to replicate the process later. This is great when your providing instructions and can be especially useful when you are providing information on topics where visual information is required, such as using a computer application.

Interactive videos
While more difficult and costly to develop than a traditional video, interactive videos can be an excellent way to deliver complicated topics or where you want to build on the learner's existing knowledge. This could be used to ask questions to test understanding, providing the learners with a choice, branching off to a different part of the video to provide a personalised learning experience. Using interactive video provides a far more engaging experience than simply watching a standard video.

Whiteboard animations
Whiteboard animations are simple videos that look as if someone is writing on a whiteboard. This is excellent for breaking down math problems, exploring topics that need both written and graphical information to make sense, and just about anything that could be taught using a real whiteboard.

Animations
Much like other forms of video, animations have gained a huge amount of popularity in recent years, while also getting much easier for normal people to make. Many animation software applications make it simple to get started with your own short animations. Of course, it is worth keeping in mind that you may need voices and music for videos like this.

No matter what type of course content you are creating, the goal is the same; to develop educational content that is engaging and effective. After all, you don't want to put hours into coursework only to have it fall flat, or for those learning from it not to grasp the most important concepts.

Interactive eLearning assets

Video is a powerful learning tool, but it is not the only learning tool and other types of assets can be created to better support the outcomes you are trying to achieve.

Interactive eLearning assets are another powerful medium that can be used in a number of ways to engage the learners. Not seen as commonly in many courses developed by coaches and consultants, interactive eLearning assets are used extensively by universities and large corporate organisations. With over a decade of experience developing content for these types of organisations, I see the power and added benefit they can bring to a learning experience.

These interactive eLearning assets can display written and visual content in a number of engaging ways, including having interactive elements that allow learners to drill deeper into content. You can also create quizzes and other interactive activities that provide an opportunity to test knowledge and experience.

Visual assets

Research shows that the human brain processes visual data around 60,000 times faster than text. In days gone by, we learned by reading books and copying chunks and passages of text, but times have changed. Based on visual design principles, digital learning experiences present an incredible opportunity to take advantage of the benefits of visual content. Pictures, illustrations, and infographics can draw the eye, capture the imagination and facilitate improved information retention. They can also help to offer digestible explanations, to break up pages of complex content and to make learning more enjoyable.

Photographs and images

They say a picture paints a thousand words. Photographs are useful for several reasons. First, they can provoke an emotional and sensory response, which compels the individual to pay attention to the image. Second photographs can simplify concepts or explanations that may be challenging to process. Our brains are programmed to retain images better than written text. According to the Visual Teaching Alliance, our brains can see images that they are exposed to for just thirteen milliseconds.

Illustrations

Illustrations are great to incorporate an abstract influence, or if you cannot find an image or a stock photo, which supports the point you are wanting to make. Being creative can also help you connect with a learner on a different level and it's an excellent way of tackling issues that are difficult to comprehend.

Infographics

Infographics are increasingly popular and can be a fantastic addition to your course content. Infographics enable you to focus on key points, to digest facts and figures and to ensure the learner goes away with an image in their head that enables them to support arguments with hard data and evidence. Research carried out by the Wharton School of Business suggests that infographics are 30-times more likely to be read than text-only content.

Presentation assets

If the program includes a synchronous (virtual or face-to-face) learning experience, then you will need to develop presentation assets. This is effectively the slides that you will be talking about when delivering your presentation. However, you may need to develop some other assets including a session plan or run sheet, which shows the timing of the delivery. You may also want to consider developing a facilitators guide, if you are looking at having other people deliver your session and you want to ensure consistency in content.

Supplementary assets

Supplementary assets include checklists, templates, workbooks, and anything else that your learners could use to record or apply their learning.

TOOLS TO BUILD YOUR LEARNING ASSETS

Creating good quality content with professional production value is important. Studies show that many people respond better to visual content than written text, so videos and images are an essential part of your content. However, visual content is only effective if the quality is excellent and poor production values will cause a lack of trust in your courses. Bad quality content can make you look amateurish, and this will cause viewers to question the legitimacy of the information in the course as well.

Designing excellent courses is obviously one of the most important things, but you also need to invest in the right tools so you can produce the course to a professional standard.

Video creation tools

When recording video content, you will need high-quality video recording equipment, lighting, editing software and much more if you want to ensure the quality of your content. Some of this equipment can be very expensive. So, it is important that you do your research before you buy.

Camera

It is essential for video creation to have the right camera for the job. A good, quality camera will help ensure that your visuals are adequately captured and allow your audience to follow your instructions better.

When creating your content, remember sound quality is more important than video quality. If the video quality is adequate, that's fine, but it is difficult for viewers to follow your content unless the sound quality is crystal clear. That is why you should spend money on audio equipment rather than an expensive video camera because you can just use your phone for video instead. Modern smartphones have advanced cameras in them, and, for most online courses, the quality is good enough.

Webcams are a great tool for recording learning assets, especially when combined with screen share tools, as you can walk viewers through the process as you do it. Webcams are also a good low-cost option, but it is important to note that many of the low-end webcams give very poor picture quality that is not adequate for recording learning assets for online courses. The built-in webcam on your laptop might be capable of handling a video conference, but the picture and sound quality will be nowhere near good enough for recording your learning materials, so if you are using a webcam, you need an external one that plugs into your laptop.

Even though smartphone cameras and webcams are adequate in some situations, you should still consider investing in a professional camera once you are established and you have sold some courses. The price and functionality of video cameras vary a lot, and if you are creating online courses, you do not need the most powerful camera out there. You do, however, need to make sure that you do not go for the cheapest option because it will not give you the quality that you need.

Microphone
The audio is a critical component of your video. You're going to need to pick up the sound clearly and concisely without any background noise or disruptions.

Lapel microphones are a great way to ensure that you get clear, crisp sound throughout your videos. Do not rely on the built-in microphones on your camera because the quality will not be as good.

Lapel microphones can be very effective if you invest in a good quality one, but you should use a desktop or boom microphone for improved sound quality and clarity. When choosing microphones for recording video, it is important to remember the law of diminishing returns. That means that a $300 microphone performs significantly better than a $100 one, but a $1000 microphone will not sound much different from a $500 one.

Lighting
Lighting is an exceptionally essential tool that will help you record your learning assets. You need to illuminate your subjects properly and ensure that there is no glare. You will want to apply the best practices in three-point lighting for optimal results.

Most times, the right lighting can be more important than the camera that you use. Even if you are going to use a slightly cheaper camera or even film videos on your smartphone, it is vital that you invest in a good lighting setup.

Teleprompter
Recording a lecture or a tutorial in an engaging way is difficult, and you can't do it all from memory, which is why you should consider investing in a teleprompter. If you do, you will find that the quality of your learning materials improves in a big way.

Video editing software
Editing is the final stage of the video creation process, and you need to make sure that you are using the right software. There will be errors that you will need to correct so that you can turn your recorded session into a final product you can actually use.

There are plenty of free options that many people find are adequate. If the features on the free video editing software are not advanced enough for your needs, you may want to consider paid video editing software instead.

eLearning authoring tools
eLearning authoring tools can come as part of an existing learning platform or as a standalone resource. With the wide range of standalone authoring tools you benefit from far more design freedoms and flexibility than built-in learning platform alternatives. Even if you are new to

learning design or authoring tools, there are a number of options to suit everyone from the design novice to the eLearning expert.

Some of the more widely-used eLearning author tools that we have had great success with include Articulate Storyline, Adobe Captivate, dominKnow One and Evolve.

Graphic design tools

There is a wide range of graphic design tools you can use to create your visual assets. There are the high-level tools used by graphic designers to create visual assets from scratch (such as Adobe Photoshop and Adobe Illustrator). Unless you have had training in these tools you would be better off with some of the simple to use drag and drop editors.

Tools (like Canva, Visme and Adobe Spark) have a range of templates, images and other graphics that gives you the power to turn an idea into a stunning graphic with ease. If you are not graphically or technically inclined, then one of these tools may be the solution for you.

Presentation tools

When we talk about presentation tools then Microsoft PowerPoint (or Google Slides or Keynote for Mac) is probably the tool that comes to mind. While this is probably the most common tool to create your presentation assets, you should also consider other tools such as the virtual delivery platform (like Zoom or Teams) if you are delivering virtually. You may also want to engage participants through polls, collaboration boards and other interactive means during the presentation and would need to have access to these tools as well.

Desktop publishing tools

Desktop publishing tools, which include things like Microsoft Word or Adobe InDesign, if you want to take it up a level, are the tools you would use to create the supplementary resources such as the checklists, templates, and workbooks.

> If you're interested in finding out about tools for creating learning content, you can jump onto our Academy at https://www.mavenzeal.academy/. We have got a free course there where we have done a lot of research into different content development tools. It is the Edupreneurs Toolkit. In this guide we provide a breakdown of the tools required to develop online content.

THE IMPORTANCE OF GOOD VISUAL DESIGN

You need to strike a good balance of visual design for your learning program because too much or too little might see you lose your students. Difficult to read text or pages packed with visual aids can make it difficult for learners to process information. But when you get the balance between your text, multimedia, layout, and everything else, your learners will be engaged with your course and find it easier to learn.

Your online learning content needs good visual design to help increase engagement, improve memory, and encourage your learners to complete the course.

Visual design principles to apply

As a course creator, you should be familiar with how to engage students using visual design principles. If you want to make your courses more engaging, then you need to apply visual design principles to your programs.

Colours

Colours play a big part in the learning process. Choosing the right colour palettes can ensure students have a greater learning experience and that they avoid eye fatigue.

Enhance your learning content by using only three colours in your design. You should also follow the 60-30-10 rule. This rule refers to using 60% of one colour, 30% of another colour, and 10% of the other colour.

Avoid using a background colour that makes it difficult to read the font or text. Choose colours that contrast together well. For example, using a dark font on a light background will provide high contrast and make the font stand out more on the page.

Typography

Do not overlook typography when creating learning content. Typography can enhance readability, help learners process information, and engage with readers' emotions.

Font styles have different effects on the reader. For example, more rounded fonts such as Comic Sans are better suited for informal topics, while Arial and Helvetica are good for easy reading. Think about your font style and whether it's relevant for the topic and audience.

If in doubt, stick to simple font styles that are easy to read and engaging. Fonts that are too fun might steal the attention away from the content or make it difficult for the reader to comprehend.

It is also a good idea to choose a combination of font styles to use. Don't use too many different styles because this can lead to a messy design. Instead, you should choose two font styles that complement each other well.

Multimedia

Multimedia includes graphics, infographics, audio clips, and videos. Eye-catching multimedia can help your reader engage with content on a different level and change their mood.

A combination of visual, audio, and textual content can work better than big blocks of text. However, you need to ensure that the multimedia content you include is relevant and provides value.

Do not overload your pages with multimedia though. People can only pay attention to one visual and one audio element at a time, so the simpler the better.

Layout and White Space

The layout of your course pages is another important visual design aspect. You want to ensure that you don't have too much or too little on the page. Overcrowding your pages with information, graphics, and texts can be difficult for your reader to digest.

When thinking about the layout, remember to include white space on the page. This helps the layout to look less cluttered.

Your text should only occupy 25% to 40% of the screen at any one time. This will ensure your content is easier to read and scan. Use visual aids to highlight where you want the reader to look. For example, using larger fonts, arrows, or different colours can help draw the reader's attention.

CRAP visual designs

Apply the CRAP design principles to create a quality visual design and positive user experience. CRAP is a design principle detailed by Robin Williams in her book The Non-Designer's Design Book, which stands for Contrast, Repetition, Alignment and Proximity.

Contrast

Contrast is one of the most important visual techniques. Contrast is "the state of being strikingly different from something else in juxtaposition or close association." (Oxford English Dictionary)

Contrast can:

- Make important elements stand out.
- Make elements that are not the same clearly different.
- Hide less important elements.
- Provide a strong focal point to attract interest.

Provide contrast in various ways by including:

- Contrasting colour, such as a colour different to other elements on the screen. This could be a different shade of the same colours or a high level of contrast between background and elements in the foreground. Using a combination of colours that lie opposite to each other on a colour wheel can also provide contrast.
- Contrasting size, such as the size of an element (text or image) being significantly larger than surrounding elements or the thickness of lines in images or text
- Contrasting shape, such as elements with disparate shapes.

Every single element of a design can be manipulated to create contrast.

Repetition
The principle of repetition means reusing the same or similar elements throughout your course. It helps to maintain consistency in your design. By repeating design elements throughout your course, you provide visual cues, so users are able to easily follow the course content and understand how it all fits together.

Elements that can be repeated to develop a sense of organisation, unity and consistency include:

- Colour, for example the same colour text for all major headings.
- Shapes, for example the same shape buttons.
- Spatial relationships, for example the same space between lines in a paragraph or between a heading and body text.
- Visuals, for example all stock photos or all vector images used in a course.
- Sizes, for example consistent size of fonts or line thicknesses in shapes or buttons.

Elements that are common across the digital space should be repeated to ensure consistency and avoid confusion. For example, hyperlinks are universally known to be blue and underlined. Creating hyperlinks with different visual elements can mean users will not understand what they are. Conversely, using blue and underline text to provide contrast when it is not a hyperlink may also create confusion.

Alignment
Alignment dictates the way every element is placed in a design. The whole point of the alignment principle is that nothing in your course design should look as if it were placed there randomly. Every element should have some connection with another element. This creates a clean and sophisticated look and feel.

Alignment can include:

- All headings being aligned the same way.
- All body text being aligned the same way (ideally left aligned, as fully justified text can pose readability issues for some users).
- Aligning all images or shapes in the same way.

Considering applying a grid when designing to ensure all visual elements are in alignment.

Proximity
Proximity is about moving things closer or farther apart to achieve a more organised look. The principle of proximity states that elements that are associated with each other should be placed closely (grouped together), and vice versa. It can

be difficult for users to identify related elements if they are spread out resulting in a poor user experience.

Examples where proximity can be applied include:

- Images and their associated captions.
- Graphs and keys on tables and charts.

Proximity can also be applied to differentiate elements, for example white space between paragraphs to differentiate between the message in each block of text.

MAKE IT ACCESSIBLE

While I am making this point last, when discussing building assets, it is far from an afterthought. When building any assets that you are using in your learning program, including the marketing assets and the systems, you need to make sure that it is accessible to everyone.

Accessible content is making sure everybody can access the learning regardless of the operating system and device they are using. This means that the learning assets are interoperable across all devices. And, that they are responsive so that a person viewing the program on a mobile device will not be disadvantaged or have any less of an experience than someone using a laptop or desktop computer.

It is also about making sure that the learning program (assets and platform) is accessible to people with disabilities. This is not just a nice to have but an actual legislative requirement that many course creators overlook. Australia (and many other countries) have adopted the Web Content Accessibility Guidelines (WCAG) as the standard for accessible online content.

The Web Content Accessibility Guidelines WCAG 2.1

The Web Content Accessibility Guidelines (WCAG) define the approaches that developers and designers should follow when creating online content – including learning programs. The success criteria are designed to support:

- Mobile accessibility.
- People with low vision.
- People with cognitive and learning disabilities.

The accessibility guidelines encourage the use of clear, consistent approaches to formatting content and the use of things like images, lists, tables and links. These approaches are, for the most part, good web design practices, but they are vitally important for people with access needs. Web content that does not adhere to the WCAG guidelines can be completely unreadable and unusable for many people.

The WCAG 2.1 has several requirements but the key elements that many course and content creators need to consider are:

- Providing text alternatives to visual media. This includes alternative text for images, and captioning or transcripts for video content.
- Making sure that any time-based media can be controlled by the user. This includes the ability to slow down, speed up, skip forward or rewind video content.
- Making content distinguishable. This includes making sure there is appropriate contrast between foreground (such as text) and background colours.
- Having content that is keyboard accessible, not requiring a mouse to navigate.

STEP 6 - SETUP YOUR SYSTEMS

Step six is all about setting up the systems to deploy and deliver. This includes the learning platform, landing pages, CRM and automations.

We've already covered a lot of the detail around this when we discussed the sixth pillar of our Blue Ocean Formula, so will not discuss all of that again. However, there are some key points to discuss about setup systems.

Landing pages and AIDA

The landing page is potentially going to be one of the first places that your prospective clients come into contact with you, your brand and your offering. To do that, we want to use the AIDA model where we (A)ttract awareness, maintain (I)nterest, create (D)esire, and get (A)ction.

Some tips for using the AIDA model when developing your landing page:

Awareness
- Keep content personal to your audience.
- Tease your audience with an intriguing headline or opening that creates curiosity.
- Use urgency that makes them want to read now - if they move on, they may never return.

Interest
- Introduce and answer pain points to strengthen the bond.
- Focus on storytelling because people still buy from people.
- Include stats, humour, and other tools that appeal to your audience.

Desire
- Be persuasive in your choice of language.
- Show how the content adds value to their career or life.
- Set your business out from the crowd.

Action
- Introduce urgency.

- Focus on clear actions.
- Use engaging CTAs.

DON'T MAKE THEM THINK

There is a great book by Steve Krug called Don't Make Them Think which discusses web usability. The principles in the book should be applied to the learning platform, landing pages, and any other web content your audience will be interacting with.

The basic premise of the book is that it should be easy for people to navigate and interact with the content. We are continually in competition for our audience's attention and if they must think, if it looks too hard, or looks like it is going to take a large investment in time then there is a greater chance that your audience will switch off and not engage.

"As a user, I should never have to devote a millisecond of thought to whether things are clickable or not."
– Steve Krug

So, when putting together your landing pages and learning platform, continually ask yourself:

- Will people know what to do?
- Will people get confused on any page?

TEST, TEST, AND TEST

One of the best ways to disengage your audience, or provide a negative experience, is to provide content that is flawed or doesn't work as expected. For this reason, when setting up the systems you need to test, test and test.

Initial testing should be done by the developer to make sure that anything inside the platform is working appropriately and operating as intended. Navigational elements are working. Videos and animations are playing when they are meant to be playing. Visual elements are appearing as required. Testing that the course flows properly and you can navigate without issue.

Next, get another person to go through the testing process as well. So often, as the developer you can get blind to mistakes which someone else might pick up.

The final part of the testing phase, is the user acceptance testing. This is where you would get your team, family, or friends to test the course. Give them a checklist of things they are meant to check and try and get enough people that you can test across different devices, operating systems, and browsers.

STEP 7 – LAUNCH YOUR PROGRAM

Finally, it's time to deploy. In this final step you deploy and deliver the course to your ideal clients in a one-to-many format.

DEPLOY

To ensure that your online course is successful, it's often a wise idea to pilot it. This is basically a way of testing it, so that you can iron out any issues before you start taking on real students. How you decide to pilot your course depends very much on the type of course. Here are just a few tips for piloting your course.

Decide how long to run the pilot

Will you pilot the course for the same time as the actual course, half the time or simply for a couple of days? The length at which you run your pilot, depends on how long the actual course is expected to last. You may be able to cram the basic elements of a long course into a few days to save you time – this won't be as costly, and it will be easier to find an audience to test on for a shorter period.

Assemble your pilot audience

Your pilot audience should ideally be complete strangers that have had no part in putting together your course.

Their opinion is then likely to be unbiased. They should be people who are interested in your course. Providing your pilot course to people at a significantly reduced rate could be a win-win for everyone.

Take notes

Once your pilot is underway, it is important to take notes so that you can spot any problems. Are your students struggling in certain areas? Are there any problems with the technology you are using? All of this is worth noting for helping you to make future improvements.

Ask questions and collect data

Asking your students questions can help you collect data on how well the course is going. This could help you to spot issues that you may not have noticed. Review analytics to see where students are spending the most time, or where they are skipping looking at certain learning objects. If you have incorporated social learning in your course, look at the quality and content of comments. This can all be done throughout the piloting process and after the pilot is complete. You can ask individuals direct questions and offer general surveys along the way.

Use your data to improve your course

Once you've finished piloting your course and collected all the data you need, you can then start tweaking your online course before its official launch. Take as long as you need to make the changes that are necessary. Once all the major flaws have been rectified and you are confident that your course is as polished as it can be, you can then finally start advertising your online course to real students.

DELIVER

Many books, articles, and training courses you read focus on the creation and selling of your online course, but often forget about the important aspect of delivering the experience.

There are many types of learning experiences that you can create, some of them very self-paced and evergreen, but the reality is that an effective and superb learning experience, that provides real impact and change requires your involvement as a coach and facilitator to guide, motivate and support your learners.

I could probably write a whole book on the delivery of an online learning experience (maybe that will be my next book) but the following are some key tips.

Be consistent when you are delivering or facilitating. This includes both in your timing and your energy. If you are facilitating an online discussion, be consistent in your presence. Being really active in the first few weeks and then dropping off means that your audience will probably do the same. The same with your energy. When we first start delivering a program our energy levels will be higher as we are excited about the new program. Try and keep that energy throughout the program.

Consider delivering to a cohort. Having everyone start and finish at the same time can help deliver a great sense of community to allow for the knowledge sharing to occur, as well as the opportunity for support from both the learning facilitator and peers.

This community driven environment enhances the learning experience by driving higher accountability, interaction, and impact. The cohort-based approach also means that most of the cohort will complete the program (due to the structure and accountability), which is going to enhance your reputation as the go-to expert in your field. It is also going to allow you to identify where knowledge and skill gaps are occurring and quickly develop new learning assets to fill those gaps. Receiving immediate feedback from the cohort also allows you to identify any technical issues or other problems that you need to address.

DEBRIEF

Once the program has been delivered, you then need to take the opportunity to debrief. There is a great image on the internet that I love. It shows the evolution of the Simpsons cartoon family from their initial designs in 1987 right through to a design from 2009. The designs are completely different and have been refined over many years. I see the design and development of the learning experience in the same way. It should be constantly evolving, adapting, and improving.

You need to constantly evaluate the success of the program and work where you can refine the program. As part of this debrief, there are five key areas to consider.

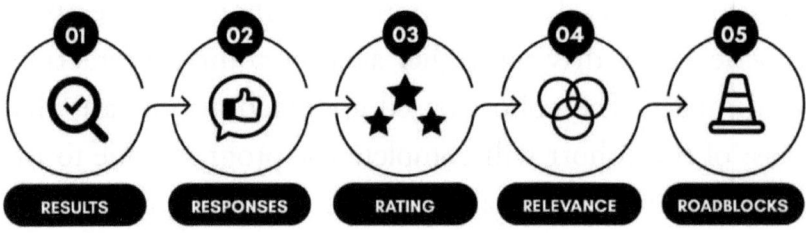

Results
The first is to look at the results the learners are achieving. Consider the big prize that your program offered. How easily are they achieving the prize? What could you do to help them achieve the prize faster, easier, or better? What could you do to improve the outcomes they are getting?

Responses
How are people responding to the information you are providing them? Are they clear on what is involved, or are they asking lots of questions to get more clarity? How are they responding to any activities you have developed?

Rating

The third part of the debrief is to gather and analyse data about the performance of the program. This could be a survey sent to all participants, or the evaluation of your Google ratings. Consider how learners are rating your program. Are you getting good ratings? What areas could you improve?

Relevance

Next, go back over the program and consider the relevance of the problem, the prize, and the steps in between. Are they all still relevant to the learners? Is the content and activities you are providing still relevant, or have things changed since you last ran the program?

Roadblocks

Finally, explore any roadblocks and determine ways to eliminate them. This could be roadblocks that participants are encountering with accessing your learning experience or roadblocks they are facing in trying to implement the learnings from the program.

CONCLUSION

So, there you have it. How you can leverage your expertise so you can scale up, create impact and live the lifestyle you desire.

As we have explored there are two key factors – the volume of clients and working one to many – that can help you move out of the red ocean and into the blue ocean, while avoiding the sinking ship and deserted island.

To achieve this, there are some key pillars including having:

- A solid strategy around why you are leveraging your expertise and where it fits into your overall business model.
- Client clarity, where you define your niche.
- A signature solution, that is going to help build credibility, provide a defined structure and ensure consistent delivery.

- An ecosystem of learning experiences to deliver interest, information, implementation and integration learning experiences.
- A selling system to move people from stranger, to suspect, to prospect, to client, to advocate.
- Technology and tools to develop and deliver your signature solution.

Developing the signature solution involves the need to:

- Nail your niche.
- Craft your pitch.
- Design your experiences.
- Promote your program.
- Build your assets.
- Setup your systems.
- Launch your program.

By following this process, you will be able to:

- Deliver impactful results.
- Scale your business.
- Have a lifestyle business.

PART X

MY STORY

---◆◇◆---

I probably would have never put myself in the position of being an edupreneur. I never thought that I would be in a position where I would be teaching or educating people. But It's funny how the path we take in life, how the natural talents that people have generally come through and guide the directions we take.

So how did I get here? How did I become the founder of a multi-award-winning digital learning agency and author on how to leverage your expertise through online learning programs?

Well, it's an interesting path I have taken to get here. I spent several years working in the horse racing industry, which is completely different to where I am now, working in the learning and development industry. I spent several years training and educating horses, and these two paths intersected while I was working overseas. During this time, I started to share my knowledge of what I was doing, working, and training with horses on to those people that I was working with.

Part of that time I spent in Japan educating young racehorses. On my return to Australia, I started work at a school in Brisbane, Queensland which was teaching Japanese students how to ride and handle racehorses. Preparing them for careers working in the racing industry. After about six months there as a riding instructor, I was asked to step into the classroom and start teaching. On my first day in the classroom, I was given the resources to train from. I remember looking at them and asking, "Is this all there is?". It was a scant volume of content, not much learning at all. The response was "Yes. Why, can you do something better?" So, I thought, you know what, I probably could. So, I started down this path of redeveloping the learning resources. At that time online was not really a thing. We had computers (I'm not that old), and I had some personal experience with computers, was fairly tech savvy so I started redeveloping several learning resources. I redeveloped all the resources for the students and moved into developing the resources for the apprentice jockeys, as well as the higher levels for a number of other theoretical subjects.

After several years, there came a realisation from the industry training bodies of each state in Australia that we were all delivering the same training and we're all developing our own resources. The decision was made for everyone to come together, to share their resources with the intention of creating a national framework of learning resources. So, we all got together over two days in Melbourne. At the end of those two days, the consensus was that 90% of the resources we're going to use were the Queensland resources. So effectively, all the resources that I had put into place, all the content that I had developed, 90% of that was going to form the national structure of training for racing industry training schools across Australia.

This made me think that, obviously, I was doing something right and this took me on the path of instructional design. I realised that I was doing instructional design, probably before I knew about instructional design, I sort of just tended to naturally gravitate towards it. So, I decided I'd continue on this path, and have now spent the last 22 years (at the time of writing this book) in the learning and development field developing online and print resources for a number of clients across a range of subject areas and industries. I decided to move on from the racing industry and needing to stay in the L&D field, I moved into the finance industry, working as a training manager for a large mortgage company. At the time, it was the second largest non-bank mortgage company in Australia.

The role I stepped into never had a training manager before, never had training resources before. So, I implemented a learning management system and started to build a suite of online resources for loan processing staff and contractors. After a while my role was changing, it was moving away from where my passion was for designing and developing learning. And after several years, I decided I needed to go out on my own. And, after a chance meeting with another training organisation, who asked me to come on and help deliver training around some learning tools, that gave me the impetus to set up my own business.

And after several years of developing training under the name of iDesign training, I went through a process of business transformation, transition and Superb Learning was born. For almost a decade we worked with large corporates, universities, registered training organisations and government departments to develop training programs for their staff and clients.

Then, in 2022 I decided to change our focus to where we are now, helping authors, influencers, and subject matter experts to leverage their expertise to help them scale, create impact, and live the lifestyle they desire. A business that is helping people along the edupreneurial journey. As part of this change, we rebranded to Mavenzeal.

Why Mavenzeal? A maven, in many languages, is a trusted expert in a particular field, who seeks to pass knowledge on to others. Zeal is defined as great energy or enthusiasm in pursuit of a cause or an objective. So Mavenzeal is a trusted expert in a particular field, with great energy or enthusiasm in pursuit of passing knowledge on to others.

This is what we are and the people we want to work with.

ABOUT THE AUTHOR

Matthew is the founder and Chief Learning Architect of Mavenzeal. Mavenzeal is a digital learning agency that helps coaches, consultants and authors to scale their business by leveraging their expertise through digital learning assets and programs.

After a career of training and educating (and falling off) racehorses, Matthew fell into training people. After realising he had a talent for designing quality training resources, Matthew embarked on a mission to further develop his instructional design skills, working in a range of different industries before starting his own learning design business. During this time, he worked with some of the biggest corporate organisations and universities across Australia and Southeast Asia, in addition to helping small and medium businesses to develop engaging learning programs.

During the COVID pandemic Matthew shifted his focus to help coaches and consultants extract their valuable intellectual property so they can scale up, create impact, and live the lifestyle they desire.

Matthew is a multi-award winning learning designer, including being recognised as the 2014 Australian Learning Impact Awards 'Learning and Development Professional of the Year'. Matthew has also been recognised as a Certified Learning Professional (CLP) and a Certified Online Learning Facilitator (COLF).

He has delivered keynotes, training workshops and panel discussions across Australia, in Singapore and the United Kingdom.

ACKNOWLEDGEMENTS

First and most importantly, I'd like to acknowledge and thank my lovely wife, Kathleen, and my children, Cameron and Caitlin, for putting up with me and supporting me as I have worked to grow the business and given me the space when I needed it to get my thoughts out of my head and write this book.

I would also like to thank my parents for their continual love, encouragement and support. Giving me the opportunities, I have had, that have worked towards making me the person I am today.

Thanks also to my wonderful clients I have worked with over the past decade or so, that have given me the opportunities to apply my skills and give the chance to learn new and different ways to design, develop and deliver superb learning experiences.

Finally, I would like to thank everyone who has purchased this book. For every book sold we have been able to further our cause of creating positive change in people's lives, by giving educational resources for seriously ill children in Australia. This has helped to ensure inclusive and equitable quality education and promote lifelong learning opportunities for all.

WORK WITH ME

---◆◇◆---

Thank you for taking the time to read this book – I hope you've found the information helpful and can use what you've learned to get the expertise out of your head, scale your business and live the lifestyle you love.

If you're serious about transforming your expertise into a profitable online course so you can scale your business and live the lifestyle you love, then we have excellent news. We are offering you a free, no-obligation session with one of our course creation experts.

During your 45-minute session, we'll discuss your current situation, what your goals are and how we can help you achieve them using our proven system.

We will also cover a stack of valuable information together, including:

- Some insights into how you can leverage your knowledge across an ecosystem of learning products.
- How you can get the knowledge out of your head in a surprisingly short time frame.
- How to avoid all the most common mistakes that coaches, consultants, and aspiring course creators make which sabotages their success.

There's no cost or obligation to move forward with our service afterwards if you feel like it's not for you. It's simply a free information session designed to educate you and provide value to you in advance.

To claim your free consultation, jump onto our website https://mavenzeal.global/ and click the link there.

Alternatively, you can join our Leverage Your Expertise membership program https://www.mavenzeal.academy/ where we have a range of online courses, structured around our Blue Ocean formula.

Or you may simply want to just stay in touch and join our Facebook community.

NOTES

LEVERAGE YOUR EXPERTISE

NOTES

LEVERAGE YOUR EXPERTISE

NOTES

Printed by Libri Plureos GmbH in Hamburg, Germany